# Hollywood, the Pentagon and Washington

# Hollywood, the Pentagon and Washington

JEAN-MICHEL VALANTIN

Anthem Press

Anthem Press
An imprint of Wimbledon Publishing Company
75-76 Blackfriars Road, London SE1 8HA

or

PO Box 9779, London SW19 7ZG
*www.anthempress.com*

This edition first published by Anthem Press 2005

First published in France by Editions Autrement 2003
Copyright © Editions Autrement 2003

The moral right of the authors has been asserted.

*British Library Cataloguing in Publication Data*
A catalogue record for this book is available from the British Library.

*Library of Congress Cataloguing in Publication Data*
A catalogue record for this book has been requested.

1 3 5 7 9 10 8 6 4 2

ISBN 1 84331 170 4 (Hbk)
ISBN 1 84331 171 2 (Pbk)

Typeset by Footprint Labs Ltd, London
*www.footprintlabs.com*

Printed in India

# CONTENTS

# ABOUT THE AUTHOR

Jean-Michel Valantin holds a doctorate in strategic studies and the sociology of defence, specializing in American strategy, and regularly contributes to the periodical *Diplomatie*. He is a researcher at the Centre for Interdisciplinary Research in Peace and Strategic Studies (CIRPES) in France and a regular visitor to Washington DC.

# INTRODUCTION: SOME KEY POINTS

During the American attack on Iraq in March 2003, a group of US soldiers was captured by the Iraqi army. Within minutes, one of them, a young recruit called Jessica Lynch, became the focus of attention of the legions of journalists embedded with the huge American war machine. A rescue operation was immediately launched to 'save Private Jessica' and her colleagues. American paratroopers stormed the hospital where the captive soldiers were being held and freed them without a shot being fired. In the hours that followed, it was announced that major Hollywood producers were interested in the idea of turning what was effectively a fairly typical skirmish into a film. This anecdote (or should we say 'episode') fits in to the world of images of what has become American warfare, images which take no account of its reality but which round it off by making it 'acceptable', by softening the blow of the formidable technological and military ease with which it can destroy any opposition in a matter of days.

Hollywood wanting to make 'Jessica's story' fits in to this reality. It is important to note that the producers proposal may have raised a smile but not really any eyebrows. This reaction shows to what extent American society, but also worldwide public opinion, has become accustomed to seeing the American strategic system and the country's film industry engage in constant communication. The key figures in the US film industry have a well-established close relationship and interdependence with the military and politicians. The evidence of this is so deep-rooted for it to be seen for what it is: a giant system where political force, military might and the power of film pervade one another and are closely inscribed in the history of American strategy, largely defining its uniqueness.

The production and practical applications of strategy cannot be separated from a specific type of movie-making that we will call here 'national security cinema'.

Even if they are markedly different, films like *Independence Day* (1996), *Armageddon* (1998), *Black Hawk Down* (2001) *Die Another Day* (2002) and many others, all take up specific themes relating to national security. The American strategic debate is depicted on screen in an extremely reactive fashion. By the power and suggestion of cinema, they cause a surge in the nation's collective consciousness of fundamental themes running through the current issues in the American strategic debate.

Films like this are made possible by the combination of monumental financial, technological and human means which are unparalleled in the world. The self-styled 'Industry' of Hollywood is the world's only cultural and industrial organization able to mobilize the resources for these national security blockbusters (whose budgets range between US$20 million and US$160 million), cutting across all genres, from war films like *Tour of Duty* (2000), to romantic comedy like *The American President* (1995). They pull in massive audiences each year, tens of millions of people and more through television repeats, DVD and video rentals and sales.

Films portraying the themes in the American strategic debate require adapted screenplays because they involve filming the nation or its soldiers and officials being put in danger. These threats can be enemy forces, terrorists, extra-terrestrials, uncontrollable machines, or even Nature herself.

This type of cinema is profoundly unique insofar as it is a precise commentary on how US production of strategy operates. In addition, whilst being extremely dramatic and spectacular, this type of cinema, like the rest of American film, arises out of a strict, sociological objective. It thus takes into account the complexity of the processes at work at the heart of this non-centralized body, the American national security system.

Herein lies the fundamental difference with France, for example, where strategic issues are largely put to one side in favour of questioning the State of the inner self of the middle classes and their secret or private lives. Questions about war, peace, security and armed aggression are also rarely the subject of cinematic portrayal. On the contrary, these subjects are given a wide berth, even forbidden, although the tide does nevertheless seem to have been turning in recent years.

In the United States, the issue of national Destiny is the subject of several cinematic traditions: the first is the Western, the story of the country's origins which makes cinema an important means of constructing the American national identity; the second is that of national security cinema, which, through detective films, war films, spy movies, science fiction and even romantic comedies, questions America's chances of survival and the legitimacy and use of her armed power, now and in the future.

The production of strategy represents a predominant collective activity that exercises the State as much as military and civilian industry, the scientific sector, universities, the media and large parts of civilian society. It results in endless power struggles between the White House, Senate Committees, the

Pentagon, the armed forces, intelligence services and military-industrial bodies. National security cinema takes into account that reality and comments upon it through on-screen dramas that can be fables about the often harsh burdens of responsibility, or even true stories exploring the use and abuse of armed force. National security films also participate in this game by taking sides with the support of the American public for or against certain prevailing ideas or official positions.

The link between the national security cinema industry and the national security State is the relationship with threat. The production of all American strategy centres around the idea of a threat that could legitimize agreements on defence and security strategies, from the implementation of large-scale weapons programmes to decisions to launch military expeditions all over the world. The American foreign policy and strategy universe is dominated by this idea of threat. For the national security elite, everything is a potential threat, from the Soviet Union to cyberspace, via retired police officers and terrorists, Third World Middle Eastern extremists or Asian 'revanchistes'. This near-obsessive perception of threat, where others might simply see differences or natural obstacles, is specific to the US national security system and at the heart of the production of strategy. It is the basis for the justification of State power and its monopoly on violence and defines its approach to other nations; cinema shows these threats and the mobilization of the means with which to overcome them.

In order to understand the meaning and evolution of national security cinema, we have to follow the development of the American strategic debate, the threats it creates and on which it depends. To tell the story of this type of cinema amounts less to a cultural and media history of the United States than to the extreme density and complexity of US strategic history. The history of relationships between the American State and strategy is also that of communication between Washington and Hollywood, which constantly transforms the application of American strategic practices into cinematic accounts. These films are at the Frontier between the history of the American national security system, American society and US culture.

The substance of this history has to be analysed along two lines: one being the gradual shift from one prevailing idea of threat to another – like that developed from 1947 onwards from Russian Communism, to that posed by Saddam Hussein in 1990, then to clandestine groups between 1993 and 2001. The second is about the levels of American strategy, which result out of an overall strategy, where the political power takes decisions according to the means at its disposal, right up to the tactical level of battle.

These twin threads are followed by cinema, which supplements strategic current affairs by films in which presidents become fighter pilots, or in which the great battles of Vietnam are replayed in order to be justified in the alternative historical universe dreamed up both by Republican party hawks or those in the Pentagon. These productions appropriate powerful symbols – armies and security agencies – and articulate them to a commentary, either obviously or subtly, on current strategic affairs. But current strategic affairs always provide the material for the constant stream of Hollywood dramas. Working out what they mean goes back to current national security issues and to America's relationship with the world and violence.

Cinema gives substance and the emotional reality of the cinematic image to the virtual Nature of strategic thinking, or to the impermanence of collective recall, by creating an alternative history, imagined and transformed into a shared spectacle which establishes a mental universe where strategic current affairs are played out, or replayed, in order to be knocked down or 'built up'.

The production of national security cinema is an extension of American production of strategy. History not being strictly linear but also synchronic, the approach adopted here is both chronological and thematic in order to take into account this complex process where strategy and the cinema industry intersect.

# NATIONAL SECURITY CINEMA AND AMERICAN STRATEGIC IDENTITY

## Structural Links

Who has not seen James Bond foil a series of transnational plots endangering the world's strategic balance; Bruce Willis destroy armies of terrorists before saving humanity from outer space menaces; Rambo end the Vietnam War by winning it; the president of the United States take charge of the Air Force to beat extraterrestrials? These films come from the United States and the drama they show on screen is sustained by the problems arising out of issues of national security.

These films are the subject of regular production, and all depict and are involved in the current issues of the American strategic debate. The American strategic debate is made up of permanent interactions (alliances, alignments but also very harsh oppositions) existing structurally between the major power bases – the White House, Congress, the Pentagon, think tanks, and the main intelligence services. The stakes of this debate are the principal choices adopted in foreign and defence policy and national security.

### From Legends to Threats

The cinema plays a full part in this strategic debate because, on the one hand, film is steeped in the main subjects that traverse it; on the other hand it puts forward an interpretation of the debate by the image. Its effectiveness resides in its implanting of founder legends like those of the 'Frontier', 'the City upon a Hill' and 'Manifest Destiny', which are the fundamental components of American identity that determine America's political and military relationship with the rest of the world.

National security cinema takes up and interprets these fundamental American legends, which give their meaning to the strategic stakes. The most powerful of them is undoubtedly that of the Frontier. Developed since the seventeenth century, this legend is that of the place where colonists settle and from which they endlessly push back the boundaries. The Frontier is an unknown, hostile place, populated by potentially dangerous natives; it is the place where the community and individual pioneers are physically and socially put to the test.

But on the Frontier, everyone is also confronted with the test of reconstructing their own identity. The pioneer is no longer dependent on nor constrained by the standards, obligations and customs that he knew at the outset. His new identity is woven by a new relationship with violence, the means necessary for survival, to appropriate land and Nature, but also to cleanse and revive himself. At the same time, the learning of this regenerative, and thus 'virtuous' violence, requires unwavering self-discipline, except when it is 'legitimate' to use it against threats which emerge on the Frontier and can be eradicated by the use of bloody, unbridled, but 'just', violence.

The Frontier legend is the memory's digest of the conquest of the West, of the building of the Nation and the repeated and legitimate use of armed force against any entity threatening the community and its rules. Even today, this tale of trial and triumph remains an emotional process, deeply implanted in the American psyche and living as a never-ending story, largely determining America's political and strategic perception of the world outside as the Frontier. The use of force in the world is thus not only legitimate but necessary, and knows no internal bounds.

This essential legend is reinforced by that of the city upon a hill, which, from the arrival of the first Puritan colonists in New England at the start of the seventeenth century, makes America the 'New Jerusalem'. The legend corresponds to the faith of these colonists in the renewal of the alliance between God and man, which makes Americans and their descendants God's chosen people. Today, this myth, and the representations which flow from it, are very much present and active in American strategic thought and the mentality of its individuals and agents of State. It confers a quasi-sacrilegious character on any attack against the United States, her interests or representatives.

These myths, representations, ideologies and symbols cut across American cinema, and particularly national security cinema, because they question the just use of force, which, at State level, becomes that of military coercion and strategic power. What is more, the myth of the New Jerusalem, which is intended to shine its light on the world, confers a singular sense on the notion of defence, which is not only that of the nation and its interests, but one of the forms of applying legitimate superiority. This theme crosses most of the main national security films. It is blatant in Roland Emmerich's *The Patriot* (2000), with Mel Gibson, where a former British army officer turned Virginia farmer joins the revolutionary army when the British army destroys his farm and kills one of his sons. He takes refuge in the forest and the swamps where he raises an army of disaffected colonists, bandits and liberated slaves. The war escalates. The British army is shown as looking to bend the colonial population to their will by terror and the sword while the governor seeks a moderate approach in order to allow the 'resumption of commercial relations after the war'.

The film ends with a battle involving the massed ranks during which the 'patriot' is the flag-bearer of the army of independence. He confronts a sadistic, bloodthirsty British officer who tortures and slaughters him in the middle of a horrifically realistic battlefield, where the victory of the pro-independents is filmed like a moment of transcendence. It is in this instant that the founder myths are invested with the construction and perpetuation of the American strategic identity: British tyranny has forced the colonists to choose between abandoning their European identity or submitting to it, and the war they lead founds their society, creating a shared feeling of threat coming from the outside. To protect themselves, they have to pass the test of living outdoors and make amends for the massacre of Indian tribes committed before the revolution. In this way, the film acts as an affirmation of American 'repentance' for the genocidal foundations of the conquest. This experience is a moment of revelation: a Utopian society can be built in America, the world can be re-founded there, because of the connection between Messianic idealism and pragmatism, particularly in a military and strategic sense.

## Political Culture

The myths of the founders cannot be separated from American political culture, to which political power is a threat in itself and should only exist by being shared between competing institutions, giving a balance of power and hence guaranteeing the freedom of citizens.

This concept of power is embodied in a non-centralized system, dominated by the 'triad' of the White House, Congress and the Pentagon. Its historic and ideological foundation is the claim of independence against the tyranny of the British Crown. It results in a general horror of tyranny, the 'mortal sin' of American political culture, which justifies all revolts, or all wars, and from which one should always defend oneself. The Federal State is thus a matrix of paradoxical representations: it represents both potential threat for the freedom of the nation and its citizens, but protects the American ideal of 'right to life, liberty and the pursuit of happiness' (the preamble to the US Constitution).

This tyrannical capacity of power is particularly identified in the military. But this *a priori* negative identification is counterbalanced by a positive one, which involves American society's affection for its armed forces, who are the effective, legitimate and heroic mechanism for protecting and defending individuals, the nation, its interests, identity, myths and values.

This opposition is expressed in the production, among others, of Roger Donaldson's *Thirteen Days* (2000), with Kevin Costner, or *Executive Decision* (1996) by Stuart Baird, starring Kurt Russell. *Thirteen Days* presents the Cuban missile crisis from a White House perspective, but depicts the military as dangerous anti-Soviet fanatics who require very close control. The film even suggests what appears to be an active resentment of certain officers towards John F Kennedy, and their rejection of the executive as the regulatory authority of their power. On the other hand, *Executive Decision* signs up to the mythology of the US army as an armed and faithful extension of American society. 'Eastern' terrorists hijack a civilian airliner and seek to blow it up over New York with a chemical weapon that could kill millions of people. Commandos from a Stealth bomber manage to get onto the plane through the hold and neutralize the terrorists. The commando unit is made up of members of every community (Whites, Blacks, Latinos, mixed race American-Asians). The heroism exhibited demonstrates the way in which the defence forces are considered an essential means of ensuring the continuation of society despite the existence of a potential threat which is always embodied in some shape or form and in this case through terrorism.

## Cinema, Threat and Strategy

American strategy is also determined by a unique relationship with the world: the United States does not have hostile neighbours, two oceans protect it from the outside world and it has never been invaded. On the other hand, the outside world is perceived as full of potential threats, and acts as an 'area of projection' of the Frontier myth by being likened to a massive Frontier-land which surrounds the United States.

The US strategic vision of the world is effectively a lot more conceptual, ideological and mythological than empirical, due to a lack of experience of the world which troubles it. The construction of American national identity operates by defining a threatening otherness, a generic 'Other'. This process is common to the vast majority of national political identity constructions; the American originality of this process comes from its material and how it is realized: the outside world is viewed according to the Frontier myth, and not through the prism of experience of invasion and counter-invasion or the flow of populations and commercial, cultural and religious exchanges.

What is more, being young and vulnerable, American society needs a consensus that the concept of a common threat supplies easily and on which the power of the Federal State relies for its development.

## Producing Threat, Creating Consensus

The production of threat is made possible through a combination of political discourse and its presentation on screen. As Michael Rogin says, threat is 'the foreign demon, the anarchist bomb planter, the tentacular Communist plot, the agents of international terrorism [who] are familiar figures of daydream which so often dominate American politicians....';[1] but it is also the fragility of the American nation against the fury of Nature, which is seen as much in a theological perspective – manifestations of God's anger – as in a strategic one – a form of unrestrained violence which must either be controlled as much as possible or survived above all. All these threats circulating in the world justify the production of strategy and military power, whose projections onto the outside world allow the imposition of American order and without which the US thinks there is no security.

The notion of threat cannot be strictly conceptual. To be effective and meaningful, it has to have an emotional dimension, to provoke genuine feelings of collective concern, even fear and horror, at the idea that destructive forces, underscored by a malevolent political ideology or will, could overturn American daily life, and wipe out its people.

During the 1950s, Hollywood constructs the Soviet/Communist threat in two ways: by extraterrestrials replacing the inhabitants of small town America, or, on the other hand, by showing massive attacks of strange, clone-like creatures, as in *The Invasion of the Bodysnatchers* (1956). In both cases, the Soviet metaphor is obvious. Today, the threat is varied. It can just as well be embodied by a group of terrorists attacking a CIA director, as in Phillip Noyce's *Patriot Games* (1992), or a media mogul wanting to start a war between China and the United States in order to boost ratings. James Bond, played by Pierce Brosnan, happily beats him in Roger Spottiswoode's *Tomorrow Never Dies* (1997).

But the threat can also emerge inside the United States, when the strategic system goes wrong and power suddenly has no opposition force. The State then puts its own society in danger, like in James Cameron's *Terminator* (1984), where the Pentagon mainframe takes on a life of its own and launches a nuclear strike against the Russians so that the retaliation gets rid of humans.

Threat is a polymorphous notion, always worked and given form by the strategic debate; it provides Hollywood with dramatic material of the highest order. The production of threat gives Hollywood the means with which to attract audiences, who in turn become a vector of public opinion because of the subjects addressed. This cross-fertilization of cinema and the strategic debate has a cyclical history, which starts at the beginning of the Cold War, with the production of threat brought about by relations with the USSR.

## Cinema and Military Identity

Films that show the defence and security community are not just simple illustrations of America's strategic preoccupations, they play a part in institutional wrangling, particularly at the heart of the Defense Department.

The US military institution has three main elements: the Army, the Navy and the Air Force, and the smaller, but immensely prestigious, Marines, who are part of the Navy. These services have a vital, organic relationship with cinema, which allows the defence forces to be linked to the great myths, the processes of political justification and the current State of affairs through the heroic portrayal of their personnel and practices.

This link dates back to 1942. After Franklin D Roosevelt invited the major film makers of the time to the White House, including John Ford and Frank Capra, in order to commission dozens of films from the standpoint of the country's psychological call-to-arms, the War Ministry set up a partnership bureau in Hollywood. The advent of the Cold War was then marked in 1947 by establishing a permanent office (the head of the partnership bureau is today Colonel Philip Straub), which consisted of setting up a certain number of organizations devoted to US security against the backdrop of the fight against the Soviet threat. In this way, the 'national security State' effectively found itself assimilated into the cinema industry and dependant upon it for its outward image, which had the effect of justifying for public opinion and for itself the production of strategy and its implementation, mostly in the form of large-scale, short-lived military expeditions.

The cooperation between the security system and the major studios functions in many and complex ways and has increased over the decades. Cooperation takes place at all stages of production: it is logistical, but also involves filmmakers, scriptwriters and actors who mainly specialize in this very particular genre. The Army may provide equipment, advisers, uniforms, training and combat hardware (from tank regiments to fighter jet squadrons and aircraft carriers). Reagan's ideological, political, technological, financial and media offensive against the 'evil empire' reinforced this trend at the start of the 1980s.

Major film-makers like James Cameron, John Milius, John McTiernan, Richard Donner, Tony Scott, Edward Zwick, Oliver Stone and Phillip Noyce dominated the gente between 1983 and 1994 by making some of the strongest films in this category, like *Rambo II* (1985) and *Rambo III* (1988), *Aliens* (1986), *Top Gun* (1986), *Predator* (1987), *Die Hard* (1988), *Glory* (1990) and *The Hunt for Red October* (1990).

These films are carried by the arrival of a generation of 'tough guy' actors specializing in 'national security roles', such as Sylvester Stallone, Arnold Schwarzenegger, Chuck Norris, Steven Seagal, Bruce Willis, Mel Gibson,

Sigourney Weaver, Denzel Washington, Morgan Freeman, Ben Affleck. All these actors are characterized by an exceptional physical presence, a singular way of embodying the might represented by powerful weapons and an ability to shoulder arms with unquestionable credibility. This cooperation is constant, but sporadic in depth, and can be distinguished as much by highs of agreement as lows of opposition.

In reality, each force decides to its own liking what support it will bring to certain films. In this way, when the Navy was still suffering from a recruitment crisis ten years after the Vietnam war, its commanders decided to support the production of Tony Scott's *Top Gun* (1986), by lending him aircraft carriers, planes and pilots and perfecting aerial choreography and new ways of filming in flight in order to make his task easier. The only condition imposed on Tony Scott was to film planes taking off and landing on aircraft carriers and combat scenes above the ocean, so as to give the film the 'Navy' stamp. The film's success was such that naval recruitment offices were set up outside cinemas which, according to the Navy, appears to have played a not insignificant role in solving the recruitment crisis. In a more bizarre way in 1978, in order to restore an image tarnished by the Vietnam War, the Navy lent a destroyer to the production company of the gay fetishist pop group The Village People for the video of *In the Navy*.

This assimilation of cinema and the armed forces is to a great extent part of the inter-service conflicts for prestige and therefore the upper hand in budgetary battles in Congress. These conflicts bring into play each force's military and strategic culture, which is linked to the element in which it operates: air, land or sea. This connection with the elements goes hand-in-hand with the very different relations to space and time which determine American concepts of war.

The Army is rooted in the land and ground combat with all that implies: suffering, blood, the heroism of pain and death, harshness and the understanding of societies they confront and either respect or destroy. The Navy is the democratic armed force *par excellence*, because a *coup d'état* can never take place on the sea; the sea is the historic medium of a strategic culture of fluidity, of the flexible diffusion of American power from the world's oceans where they have a constant presence and are capable of encircling lands while ensuring their vital trade routes are secure. The marines are the affirmation of the Navy's historic ability to go ashore and open up the land to non-maritime troops transported by ship. As for the Air Force, it is the aerial deployment arm, free from terrestrial contingencies; it is characterized by the fusion of man, equipment and technology in the experience of flight. It transcends distances, gives an abstract character to borders and demands not only courage and reason but also tenacity and speed. The aerial concept of war is characterized by temporal contraction, the extreme vulnerability of its crews and the ideal of incapacitating land and sea defences; it has a tendency to make the idea of ground combat obsolete.

These peculiarities of military identity are perfectly reproduced by cinema, especially since 1995 and the 'Revolution in Military Affairs' (RMA), a plan to transform the American military machine by technology and a synergy between equipment that targets and processes information and larger, more rapid projection capabilities. This global change in the concept of military function markedly revitalized cinematic competition between the armed forces. Since 1995, we have been witnessing a symbolic and ferocious struggle between the Air Force, which, through images, is ensured tactical and strategic primacy of *air power* and *space power*. The struggle presents itself as the way in which the ideal of 'global reach' can be attained, in other words, the ability to project forces anywhere in the world in a very short space of time. The theory of 'global reach' made its appearance not long before the Gulf War.

On the other hand, the Navy claims to be the best at being able to control the flow and movement of troops and really significant material because of the amount of tonnage it can muster.

This conflict is expressed in the increasing number of 'Air Force films' and 'Navy films'. Thus, in 1996, in Roland Emmerich's *Independence Day*, with Will Smith, the Air Force saves the Earth from extraterrestrials. Similarly in 1997, Ridley Scott's *GI Jane*, starring Demi Moore, proclaims that the United States international security depends above all on the quality of its Navy personnel and the ability to get them to intervene anywhere in the world, the Navy being permanently on hand from one coast or another.

However, these inter-service conflicts, by extending themselves into cinema, thus acquire a deeper significance which transcends them in the name of national security: they allow them to participate in the production of threat (which itself justifies their existence) and the production of strategy.

The cooperation between civilians and the military brought about by the existence of this type of cinema can have unexpected consequences. During the filming of James Cameron's *Abyss* (1989), new types of underwater cameras were developed which were then adopted by the Navy.

## Creating a Mental Universe

Being part of both the strategic debate and the commercial requirements of the big studios, national security cinema creates a mental universe where the dramatic imagination and American strategic culture combine.

As entertainment, national security cinema is not restricted to the auditorium, but, like the whole of the American film industry, infiltrates the private sector through cable and satellite television or the video market. The collective impression left by the films is equally created by repeats of trailers which amount to national marketing campaigns, to such an extent that it is often impossible to ignore the distribution of certain films. There were formidable marketing and distribution campaigns in this way in 1999 and 2002 for episodes one and two of George Lucas *Star Wars*, *The Phantom Menace* and *The Attack of the Clones*. The long wait for these films, which are deeply rooted in American mass and strategic culture, was cultivated and used in order that the films distribution coincided with a publicity campaign and the sale of numerous spin-off products (toys, clothes, video games, books, drinks, magazines, billboards, posters). These two campaigns, impressive by their sheer size, are hardly isolated cases in the history of national security film promotion. Similar methods were employed to maximize the prestige of films like *Rambo II*, *Terminator II*, *Independence Day*, *Die Another Day* and *Mission: Impossible*. Since 1987 and *The Living Daylights*, James Bond films have furthermore become massive advertising mediums for different cars, watches, perfumes, jewels and other luxury items.

However, only talking about 'simple' marketing would be to forget that this commercial deployment comes in a variety of forms and supports the particular mental universe of the collective US imagination with regards to national security. Unlike the mentality of European cinema, which has, after 1,500 years of civil war and international conflict, contemptuously rejected and even denied war and the passions it gives rise to, American cinema seizes on the national preoccupation for war, strategy, weapons and a certain fear of the outside world. The American mentality steadfastly keeps alive the issue of the battlefield, its sectors and categories. As Sun Tzu wrote, 'The Art of War is of vital importance to the State. It is a matter of life and death, a road either to safety or to ruin. Hence it is a subject of inquiry which can on no account be neglected'.[12]

For Americans, war, the army and the politics of power relations do not correspond to historical experience, but represent a constant mental reference point. They are in effect the vehicle for and the benchmark of the problem of protecting a society imbued with the sense of its own vulnerability and finiteness, at the same time as a conviction of being the guardian of a 'manifest Destiny' which must be defended by force when the need arises. National security cinema responds to the American strategic culture by giving form to these ideas and fears. The US mentality is predisposed to military spectacle, to admiring weapons and technology but not to point of adoration; weapons are also a source of fear and defiance because they embody the risk of wrenching from the individual the essential values of freedom, democracy and the law.

This ambivalence is analysed by Alexis Bautzmann[3] as one of the essential forms of the American mentality; he compares it to the 'guile', the 'ruse' of the Greeks, of which the archetype is Ulysses – not only is he king of Ithaca, but also a warlord and a man able to master and even hijack technology, notably with the construction of the Trojan horse. A man full of 'cunning' is able to employ technique to his advantage without becoming a slave to it and, if need be, to fight with all his strength to survive and destroy his enemies. The means employed to do this, including weapons, can thus be ones of liberation and victory as well as of threat. The 'good' hero, from the American point of view, is both a technologist but also close to Nature.

Characters like Rambo who transform the environment into a weapon against their enemies, oil workers who blow up an asteroid in *Armageddon*, commandos who cobble together anti-tank bombs in the midst of battles against the Germans in *Saving Private Ryan*, all attest, in different ways and to varying degrees, to the same 'heroic ruse', between the artisan, resourcefulness and the mastery of the latest technology, which allows the individual to reverse situations where, on the face of it, the odds are stacked against him.

This type of cinema acts as the medium between the different authorities of strategy and US make-believe; these very dense and complex relationships have a history, which is that of the American strategic debate since the end of the 1940s.

# 2

# EXPERIENCING AND DREAMING UP HISTORY, 1951–1982

Relations between the cinema industry and the national security system depend on the rapport maintained by public opinion and 'grand strategy' – the level at which political decisions connect with the means of realizing it. Cinema being a private venture, it is only reliant on the national security system when the opinion of the public, whose members make up its clientele, matches policy.

Relations between the two from the Second World War to the death of John F Kennedy are determined by a long cycle of alignment of these three authorities (grand strategy, cinema, public opinion), apart from certain sudden adjustments, including the period of McCarthyism at the start of the 1950s. National security cinema at this time is an illustration, produced at an industrial rate, of the Communist threat, but also an examination of the nuclear deterrent, which is exposed as impossible to justify when its genocidal crudity is captured on film.

## Military Logistics at Hollywood's Service

At the start of the 1960s, relations between Hollywood and the Pentagon were so healthy that they led to the production and filming of *The Longest Day* (1962), under the direction of Ken Annakin, who mobilized the vast majority of Hollywood's leading lights. The film required a logistical deployment of such a size from the Army and the Navy that, in a real high point, it led to the *ad hoc* creation of a 'military-cinema' unit ensuring the promotion and legitimization of the US presence in Europe, ten years after the creation of NATO. This organization paved the way for a series of military blockbusters in the 1960s and 1970s such as the *Battle of the Bulge* (1965), *Where Eagles Dare* (1969), *Tora! Tora! Tora!* (1970) about the Battle of Pearl Harbor, *Patton* (1970) or the *Battle of Midway* (1976). Each one of these productions, which needed massive military means, would not have been made without the logistical help of the Navy and the Army.

All these films proceed on the basis of the Second World War being a 'good war'. It is just, led heroically in the Pacific against bellicose and anti-democratic imperialism, and in Europe against Nazism, the modern form of evil.

It involves perpetuating a tradition embodied in a great number of productions started during the war itself and continued into the 1950s. They present the military in war as the extension of the nation and the accomplishment of each soldier-citizen in absolute adversity when threatened with death in combat, by overcoming his fears and summoning up his courage and faith in the collective and individual Destiny.

## Cold War and Science Fiction

This period extending from the origins of the Cold War to the start of the 1960s also saw the confirmation of cinema's capacity to produce threat, by aligning itself to the definition that prevailed in the strategic debate, and thus became the essential means through which threat was spread at national level. It was in this strange parallel universe created by the image industry that the invasion of the United States by extraterrestrials began.

The first important film, among dozens of others, was *Destination Moon*, in 1950. It depicts a group of American scientists who take advantage of a moon landing to establish a US base, before 'the others' install nuclear weapons. Furthermore, the film adopts in this way the Air Force line, which was still pushing calling for more funding in research and development as well as the monopoly of using nuclear weapons.

As in the rest of society, this discourse coincided with a sudden wave of paranoia at the highest level of the State, of which the tragedy of the Secretary of State for Defense, James Forrestal, was a striking example. Blessed with a prodigious capacity for work, Forrestal, the high-ranking Secretary of the Navy, was one of the first and most passionate anti-Soviet zealots. For some reason, an increasing terror ate away at him from within, to the point where he was arrested in the middle of the night on the streets of Washington DC, shouting: 'They're coming, they're coming!' He committed suicide in hospital several days later.

The start of the 1950s was marked by the spread of the 'civil defence' ideology, which was given substance and promoted by radio and television programmes, press articles and works of fiction – all supported by the Federal Civil Defense Agency – inciting society to prepare themselves for the consequences of a possible Soviet nuclear attack by constructing shelters and learning a socially useful skill, forged by adhering to a common vision of threat.

The national security elite perceived the world as the place in which the threat of Soviet power was played out. This vision, crystallized in the higher realms of the State, was broadcast to the wider public at the national level of ideas and representations via the media and the political and education system, invalidating the myth that the federal State has little influence over the development of American society.

Hollywood was brought into this gigantic mechanism, in particular by producers who were aware of the capacity for political interference following the redoubtable period of McCarthyism (1949–1953), with its black lists and denunciations on the pretext of Communist sympathies. Scriptwriters, who were receptive to the dominant trends of the national imagination and the pervading atmosphere of crisis, went along with and heightened the movement. They benefitted at the same time from the more or less discreet support of organs of State liaison between Washington and Hollywood. The 1950s were thus not only a 'propaganda plot', but an immense example of the realignment between State and society, notably through the cinema industry, national security ideology, and a collective sense of threat.

This State of affairs was expressed in the production of numerous science fiction films, like Christian Niby's *The Thing From Another World* (1951), where an Arctic base is invaded by an extraterrestrial killer, Robert Wise's *The Day the Earth Stood Still* (1951), where galactic police demands that Earth stops engaging in war on pain of destruction, or even *When Worlds Collide* (1951), in which a space Noah's Ark is constructed in order to save certain carefully selected sections of humanity before the destruction of Earth by a meteorite. All are based on the same problem of an imminent danger threatening to strike the United States and destroy it.

A large number of films from this era participate in the construction of a national consensus around national security policies and strategies, due to the institution of a consensus in society on themes stemming from the Soviet Communist threat. It was the era of *cold war cultural consensus*.

Wolf Rilla's *Village of the Damned* (1960), based on John Wyndham's best-selling science fiction novel, *The Midwich Cuckoos* (1957), is particularly representative of this process, with its projection of Communist plot signifiers, psychological pathology, contagion and subversion, all presented as a sort of perfect threat. The film starts with a UFO passing over the small town of Midwich. Nine months later, all the women give birth at the same time. The children are strange, almost clone-like creatures, who communicate between themselves by telepathy, impose their will on adults and push those they find threatening into committing suicide. They form a parallel society, ruled by a community spirit. The primary schoolteacher then learns to disguise his thoughts by imagining a brick wall. He prepares an attack. He sets fire to his school, sacrificing himself and destroying all the monster children.

This film is a textbook example of cinema's treatment of the Communist threat. At the start, it paints a picture of an everyday social ideal corresponding to American values of accomplished individualism. Everyone is self-disciplined, pleasant, respectful of their neighbours private lives and of the civic life of the community where mass consumption triumphs. Husbands are at the office, wives in modern fitted kitchens. The UFO's flight over Midwich is a metaphor and a euphemism for the mass rape women are subjected to when besieged cities fall, but it also has sufficient religious resonance by showing an 'anti-Immaculate Conception'.

The unborn children from this moment bear the mark of the strange, the barbarous invader and the Antichrist. They represent the sudden emergence of a deeply-altered collective identity at the very heart of the fundamental means of biologically and anthropologically continuing society. Implicitly, the threat the children of Midwich bring to bear on the town is the slow death of all inhabitants who do not accept the new totalitarian norm of social life. The children symbolize the threat of Communist subversion which would impose a system of values at odds with the Messianic identity of America.

The primary schoolteacher's reaction takes hold both at the time in the ideology of *civil defence*, but also, in an equally bleak fashion, in the seventeenth century where, witches – women who were not subject to the law of preachers but guardians of a European culture and an ancestral, rural religion, living secretly according to a non-Christian mentality – were mercilessly hunted down and burned at the stake.

It follows from this that the US idea of threat is a continuum between political and religious make-believe with threat being the ideological, political and undoubtedly demonic adversary all at the same time. The American mentality is not the French one; the US has not experienced 'disillusionment with the world' (Max Weber). But the production of threat and its on-screen representation by Hollywood is not just about the outside enemy. The process also affects the internal pillar of American strategic security – military nuclear power and deterrent from 1954 onwards.

## Nuclear Deterrent as Threat

A tradition of strategic and cinematic thought was born with the bombings of Hiroshima and Nagasaki which challenged the legitimacy of nuclear weapons as a guarantor of the security of the United States. President Dwight Eisenhower formalized the first doctrine of nuclear deterrent, called the 'doctrine of massive reprisals', based on the idea that any attack, of whatever size, on the United States or one of its allies by the Soviet Union, would lead to a massive use of nuclear weapons in response.

One cannot conceive of defending oneself against nuclear weapons because their speed cancels out the dialectic of attack and defence that makes war possible. What is more, the direct and varied effects of nuclear weapons, the size of the explosion then the fall-out, can prevent power being reproduced, even the social and biological reproductive capabilities of a bombed society being a viable one. It thus involves a potential death sentence for the Soviet Union. But, equally, the Soviet Union was equipped with similar capabilities, and the game of reciprocal deterrent was founded on the guarantee of mutual destruction.

Despite its effectiveness, nuclear deterrence would never be popular. On the contrary, public opinion, numerous political bodies and the cinema viewed this ever-expanding power as a threat in itself, far worse than that which the 'international Communist conspiracy' and the Soviet Union brought to bear. This mistrust was formalized and popularized by cinema from the mid-1950s with 'monster films', of which the most famous, *Them!* (1954) by Gordon Douglas, portrays and attack on Los Angeles by giant ants that have mutated through radioactive fall-out from nuclear tests. Despite its relatively short shelf-life, the message this genre sends out is that nuclear weapons are a perversion of power and are expressed through the transformation of Nature into a dangerous and grotesque object.

It must be noted furthermore that, at the same time, Japanese cinema was being overrun with Godzilla films and their spin-offs, like useless *Mothra*, portraying gigantic monsters created by radioactivity which devastate entire towns, either by destructive madness or when they are confronted. If this type of Japanese cinema were part of a series of political, social and cultural processes attempting to go back to the trauma of Hiroshima, it is clear that the horror inflicted on Japan had been perfectly integrated by those in charge of strategy and cinema in the United States and was feeding the fear of the US suffering the same fate. But if one was trying to harness horror and trauma as a way of avoiding conflict, the other was warning of its fundamentally illegitimate Nature, that risked taking hold in American towns as it had done Japanese ones.

Monstrous creatures are also metaphors for the unleashing of forces that are no longer either natural nor technological but monstrous and 'Promethean'. They defy all control, putting in danger the material framework of American urban civilization, the symbol for US citizens that they have left the world of Nature and therefore the Frontier.

In another way, the start of the 1960s was dominated by the dramatization of the possible effects of a nuclear war, or the way in which it could be started. In 1959, Stanley Kramer directed *On The Beach*, based on the novel by Nevil Shute and starring Gregory Peck and Ava Gardner. The film follows the crew of a submarine which has taken refuge in Australia following a nuclear war. The world is little more than a radioactive ruin and the winds are pushing the radioactive clouds slowly towards Australia. The film shows the tragedy of the last days of humanity, through a doomed love affair between the submarine captain and an Australian woman while her fellow countrymen and women kill themselves. This problem is taken up and extended in a very black, yet humorous, fashion by Stanley Kubrick in *Dr Strangelove* (1963). The director dissects the fragility of the nuclear balance by showing an Air Force colonel, overcome with anti-Communist paranoia, taking it upon himself to order a squadron of B-52 bombers from Strategic Air Command (SAC) to bomb the Soviet Union. The film follows the efforts of the military command and the president to recall the planes and avoid a crisis with the Russians, helped by the cynical counsel of a former Nazi turned adviser on nuclear strategy. The film ends on the executive and military powers' decision to seek refuge in underground complexes with women while the world blows up.

It could be said that Peter Watkins' *The Bomb* (1965) continues Kubrick's aims. The film is intended to be a 'documentary fiction'; it follows the breakdown of English society after a nuclear exchange. The population of London is slowly poisoned by the fall-out from this attack, but also starved, and the government calls in the troops. The film ends with the soldiers putting those who are dying in the streets out of their misery with a bullet to the head.

We go from tragedy to fable with Franklin J. Schaffner's *The Planet of the Apes* (1968), starring Charlton Heston in an adaptation of the novel by Pierre Boulle. An American astronaut lands on a strange, barren planet, where monkeys speak and live in a very sophisticated society and where man has regressed just short of articulated speech. A 'hard-line' faction of militaristic gorillas and orangutans and sophist, scientistic priests campaign to kill all humans. Having escaped their clutches, the hero steps out onto a long beach and suddenly notices the remains of the Statue of Liberty, half-buried in the sand. He collapses, shouting: 'Ah, the fools, the fools, they launched the bombs!'

This series of films, which inspired dozens of others on a lesser scale, show the irrevocable Nature of nuclear war. For film-makers, the nuclear argument appears irreparably synonymous with the destruction of civilization, if not humanity.

This horror inspired by the nuclear deterrent, because of the unvoiced comment that goes with it, was carried through the 1970s and into to the mid-1980s, where films like *Rollerball* (1975) and *Logan's Run* (1976) put forward the argument that the aftermath of nuclear conflict will lead to the emergence of totalitarian regimes in the United States. Nevertheless, if, in the case of nuclear weapons, the studios do not align themselves with official positions, there is no fracture between the cinema industry and political power. Things change with the Vietnam War.

## The Vietnamese Fracture

The Vietnam War will effectively sow deep trouble in the ways in which the production of threat, films and strategy are linked. Between 1964 and 1967, American involvement in Vietnam was bogged down in a conflict whose objectives were unclear; while the violence increased, the certainty of victory faded and American society was more and more fiercely divided about the question of war.

From 1966, the strength of society's internal opposition to American strategy mounted. It is against this backdrop that in 1965 John Wayne, drawn by reading Lewis Milestone's novel *The Green Berets*, wrote to President Johnson to tell him how important it was for the American people to understand the reasons for the US engagement in Vietnam. He suggested 'telling the story of our troops with truth, emotion, strong characters and action. We want to do it in such a way that we will inspire a patriotic attitude in Americans, a feeling that has always roused us in this country in periods of tension and crisis.' President Johnson reacted by urging the Pentagon to provide helicopters and advisers, at a cost of up to several million dollars. The film, also called *The Green Berets*, was filmed in 1968 by John Wayne himself. With flamboyant militarism, it constitutes an apology for the fight waged against Communism in Vietnam by the American Army. This hard-line propaganda film, which reflected the unilateral positions of the administration, found its way on to cinema screens just after the Tet offensive in January 1968. This offensive had a hard-hitting impact on American public opinion, who suddenly understood that their *boys* were involved in a never-ending war.

There followed a radical shift in attitude in Hollywood in relation to the war. It immediately found expression in the same year, with the distribution of Sam Peckinpah's *Wild Bunch*, a crepuscular Western of a violence hitherto unseen and which has not been matched even today. It shows the massacre of the Mexican army by a gang of terrifying old American outlaws in an orgy of armed violence. At the end of the massacre, the Pueblos Indians, who repel all invaders in the mountains by using the terrain to their advantage, retrieve weapons from among the piles of bodies, and become even more dangerous – an obvious allegory for the Viet Cong.

This Western was in keeping with the change of opinion in Hollywood against the Vietnam War: because of financial necessity, studios could not allow themselves to go against public opinion. In addition, like the rest of the country, opposition to the war cut through Hollywood and particularly inflamed the liberal and educated elite, including cinema industry representatives (actors, scriptwriters and producers) who were helping to guide this tide of opinion.

While the Vietnam War ended bitterly in 1975 with American troops, diplomats, the secret service and their paramilitary teams leaving Saigon, Vientiane and Phnom Penh in a hurry, abandoning territory and their local allies, Francis Ford Coppola had been working on the production and filming of *Apocalypse Now* for a year.

Because of his previous successes, including *The Godfather* (1971), Coppola had acquired the necessary political weight inside the studios to pitch for and have accepted the finance for his projects. *Apocalypse Now*, despite its Pharaonic dimension, was accepted by Universal. For the first time since the Second World War, an extremely large-scale war film was produced without the support of the American army.

Taking inspiration from Joseph Conrad's novel *Heart of Darkness*, *Apocalypse Now* relates the voyage of a special forces officer through different circles of hell while on a mission up the Mekong river to Cambodia. He has orders to kill a paratroop colonel who has raised his own army and carved out a warrior kingdom for himself. During the voyage, Captain Willard witnesses the pointless destruction of the Vietnamese population and civilization and the deportation of peasants, while the American army collectively sinks deeper into madness, the absurd and the horror. His encounter with Colonel Kurtz is the moment of revelation about the sources of American failure: the US war effort found itself up against an enemy imbued with a spirit of sacrifice such that any attempt to break it required committing evil and accepting horror and suffering for itself with a tenacity that completely surpassed that of the Americans, or even to resort to the ultimate taboo – nuclear weapons. Colonel Kurtz has fallen into madness by dint of immersing himself in cruelty and evil, the rural and mystical forms of which he has created among his followers are the counterpart to America's consumerist military frenzy.

In this way, *Apocalypse Now* makes the Vietnam War the collective experience of evil in the name of the grand strategy of the fight against Communism. This quasi-damnation of the American army equates, on an individual level, to damning its soldiers, who, as conscripts, represent the middle and disadvantaged classes of American society. The breakdown of social links, sense of individuality and the rise in madness and oblivion on board a boat going up river is a discourse on the effects of war and strategy on American society.

Francis Ford Coppola was forced to go the Philippines to produce his film and hire the equipment for certain legendary scenes, in particular helicopters, from the Philippines army during the Marcos dictatorship, who was, it should be added, supported by the CIA and the State Department at the time.

The Vietnam experience thus also split the 'military-cinema unit' into two opposing camps: a conservative one that spoke to the 'silent majority' defined by President Nixon, and the liberal perspective that virulently denounced the conflict, its social and ideological effects, as well as the political and strategic system that supported it.

This second perspective prevailed during the second half of the 1970s until the election of Ronald Reagan. It worked on the divisions that tore apart the national security system at the political level because of Byzantine conflicts that pitted the White House against the Pentagon, the CIA and the State Department. These conflicts sparked two major crises: the discovery of a Navy spy in the White House, then the Watergate scandal. The presidencies of Nixon, Ford and Carter were marked by the spread of the Vietnam War into Cambodia in 1969, the CIA's organization of General Pinochet's *coup d'état* against Allende in Chile in 1973 and the inability to dissuade the USSR from invading Afghanistan in 1979. The result was a serious political mistrust of the institutions in charge of the defence and security of the nation. This was seen in several inquiries led by Congress to control the CIA and by a serious recruitment crisis, whereas the American army had to confront powerful internal tensions.

This mistrust was illustrated and maintained by the liberal wing of Hollywood. The symbolic national security film of this era was Sydney Pollack's *The Three Days of the Condor* (1975), starring Robert Redford. One fine morning, a CIA monitoring station falls victim to a surprise attack by an unknown commando unit. Only one analyst escapes, by chance. He investigates the situation while continuing to hide from the mysterious killers. He then discovers secret plans to invade oil-rich states in the Persian Gulf to prevent them falling into the hands of the Soviets. He realizes that the order to destroy his department is the result of a misunderstanding at the political level of the secret service. He then looks for a way of lifting the lid on the war plans scandal, but his journalist contact has an 'accident', whilst the representative of the 'moderate' branch of the CIA makes contact with him and reminds him that it is both normal and necessary for a great power like the United States to prepare this type of operation, even if it does not taken place. At the end of the film, alone and abandoned by everyone, the hero – a kind of 'last honest man' – appears to be assured of certain death.

This work deepened the division between public opinion and national security by clearly demonstrating the anti-democratic Nature of institutions who owe nothing to any legitimately elected, political authority and are a potential danger to the freedom of individuals. This problem of mistrust towards national security was taken up again in Richard Donner's *The Omen* (1976), starring Gregory Peck and Lee Remick. The United States ambassador to Rome, then London, is destined to be the next US president. He adopts a child who is in fact the Antichrist and is protected by a conspiracy destined to secure his political future. The two follow-ups to *The Omen* show Damien, the child of Satan, entering West Point and inheriting his uncle's industrial empire, before being appointed ambassador to London and preparing for nuclear war against the Soviets. The film clearly depicts the apocalyptic fantasies triggered off by the existence of nuclear weapons and also contains a discourse on the receptiveness to evil of the foreign political elite and American oligarchies. In the United

States, politics is never free from theology (remember that the president has to swear on the Bible to respect the Constitution), and the reaction to this theological and political mentality in nuclear strategies was none other than an upsurge in millenarianism which envisages the end of the world as a certainty.

This disqualification of the American strategic system coincided with the production of important films, including *The Deer Hunter* (1978) by Michael Cimino and Martin Scorcese's *Taxi Driver* (1976), about the suffering of soldier-citizens whose experience of war has tipped them over the edge into madness and nihilism.

## The Reagan Revival

The threatening trend in American political and ideological history, however, was marked by a refusal of extremes and the demand for consensus, which explains the change in direction of film producers at the beginning of the 1980s, during Ronald Reagan's first term at the White House.

*Rambo* re-established the good relations between the strategic system and cinema, even giving cinema the chance to say its *mea culpa*. *Rambo*, filmed in 1982 by Ted Kotcheff, starring Sylvester Stallone and Richard Crenna, is the story of a decorated former Green Beret and Vietnam War veteran who is arrested by the police in a small town while he looks for a place to eat after learning of the death of his last comrade-in-arms. Harassed, humiliated and physically and morally tortured, he eventually reacts; his conditioning as an elite soldier re-emerges and his reflexes gain the upper hand: he batters the police officers to death and flees into the forest. Hunted down, he embarks on Guerilla warfare which becomes a small regional conflict when the national guard are called in. Finally, he wreaks havoc on the 'small quiet town'. Holed up in the police station, he is reunited with his former colonel, spiritual mentor and father figure, who asks him to give up his weapons. Rambo explodes with rage, screaming that since his return from the war, he has been shouted down, ignored and marginalized, despite having fought and gone through hell for those who, on his return, have treated him as a 'baby killer'. The last sequence sees Rambo, escorted by the colonel, leaving the building surrounded by police officers. Unlike the book on which it is based, the film does not end with Rambo being killed by the State police.

The whole of this powerful film, carried by an exceptional actor, has as its strategic problem society's error in rejecting their army by stigmatizing it as criminal and refusing even to admit that it obeyed an elected power. This injustice is a factor in the lack of understanding, resentment and division which is resolved only when violence makes way for speech: speech re-establishes the democratic link between citizens, but also between political and defence institutions. Rambo carries the cry of rage and suffering of the defence community who have been rejected by those to whom they have dedicated themselves.

This turnaround was concomitant with, without being dependant on, a major ideological movement, that of Ronald Reagan's 'conservative revolution', whose slogan, 'America is back', symbolized a new relationship with history and the country's own image. The 'return' it concerns dates back to the adoption, pushed through by the hawks of the Reagan team, of a very offensive position against the Soviet Union and the collective fantasy of decline that characterized the United States from the beginning of the 1970s.

## Supplementing History by Daydream

In this way, the cinema industry latched on to the relationship with history. Military and political history since the death of John F Kennedy having been that of defeats and a loss of legitimacy, the image factory worked on producing an imagined history. American strategic recall had been subjected to such trauma with the Vietnam War that it suffered a mental block on the episode and was unable to assimilate it and mourn its loss. This war remained an open psychological wound which maintained a collective feeling of vulnerability and identity crisis. Whilst American identity has been constructed since the seventeenth century around the idea that America and its settlers are God's chosen people and that their manifest destiny is to illuminate and guide the world towards its redemption and salvation, the Vietnamese trauma blurred American self-perception; it threatened to deeply harm the collective identity by its character as an 'unjust war' which risked reducing the United States to the level of 'simple' superpower, not Messianic, but coldly hegemonic, capable of experiencing defeat, in other words, decline.

Against this historical and existential anguish, American cinema created a world of images, ideas and ideology which overturned the negative relation with history. It all started in 1983 with Ted Kotcheff's *Uncommon Valor*, starring Gene Hackman. The film begins with one of the most impressive war scenes ever filmed: American soldiers, pounded by mortar shells and pursued by the Vietcong, are running towards helicopters. Those at the front manage to get on board but the aircraft have to take off in the great rush and the horrified survivors watch their comrades abandoned on the ground. The rest of the film shows the organization of a private rescue operation by the father of one of these soldiers, diplomatic efforts to recover those missing in action having failed. He assembles a group of veterans and two helicopters and leaves to attack a prisoner of war camp. The remaining soldiers are saved and the father learns that his son died some months beforehand, after caring for and saving several of his companions.

This film makes American history a cycle, which resumes its course after being interrupted in 1975, by declaring that even though American troops have withdrawn from Vietnam, the war is not over. It has been suspended to be resumed and finished by the dream of victory in the alternative reality of cinema.

In this film, the victory is first of all ethical, it is about rehabilitating the soldiers' memory and reuniting families, if only by making it possible to start the grieving process for the 'lost son'.

But military victory is soon declared in Joseph Zito's *Without A Trace*, starring Chuck Norris in 1984. It again involves rescuing prisoners, forgotten by a former officer. However, the difference with Ted Kothceff's film is that the emphasis is not on the veterans' recovery of their dignity but on the war waged by Colonel Braddock against the Vietnamese army with the liberation of the prisoners as the unambiguous measure of victory. In addition, Colonel Braddock's tactics are about using terrain, encirclement, ambush and surprise attack, which are all acquired from the Vietnamese. The film affirms the US army's capacity to learn, adapt and use the enemy's own skills against them.

This interpretation of the present as a supplement, perfecting the past, and the engagement of cinema in a supporting role in the healing process of American strategic recall and identity allowed the creation of an alternative, virtual reality where history was replayed and a Reagan-like reconstruction of American pre-eminence in the world operated. This ideal reality was enhanced in 1985 by *Rambo II*.

Rambo, imprisoned, finds himself asked to return to Vietnam in order to find proof that American prisoners are being held. Betrayed by the CIA, he is captured by the Vietnamese and discovers that the Soviets are assembling an elite group of soldiers to control Vietnam and destabilize South-East Asia. Sublimating himself in the ordeal of treason, torture, grief and survival, Rambo becomes a modern Titan, exhibiting his strength in water, on land and in the air against Vietnamese–Soviet patrols; after freeing the prisoners, he deluges the Soviet camp with torrents of fire and steel. He will then declare his desire for justice for those who sacrificed their lives for the love of a nation which denies the enormity of their sacrifice.

The creation of this alternative historical reality relaunched the synergy between Hollywood and the national security system, who were reconciled by their offensive against the common threat of the Soviet 'evil empire', which acted as a matrix as much for the dialectic movement which makes history as for the production of strategy and film since 1945.

# 3

# JUSTIFYING THE NEW
# STRATEGIC POWER, 1982–1990

In order to give substance to the vision of America's 'return', President Reagan, his team and the instruments of power which support him had to maintain that the country was faced with major ordeals, comparable in size to that of the United States.

The negative image the United States had created for itself since Vietnam was corrected by the creation of a virtual threat which, while being rejected outside America, allowed a call-to-arms for its security and defence. In addition, being confronted by a symmetric threat could only justify again the national security machine's existence and its large budgets, all of which experienced unprecedented inflation during Reagan's first term of office.

## Ronald Reagan and Threat: New Threats from Old

In this way, the idea of the Soviet threat reappeared and was set out from the start of the presidency as an uninterrupted discursive strategy. One of its most celebrated occurrences was the famous speech of 16 March 1983 before American evangelical preachers on the need to fight the 'evil empire'. In an almost prophetic tone, Ronald Reagan rekindled the New England puritans' vision of the world, who viewed it as the place where Satan and his allies were at work and where the virtuous man proves his worth by fighting them.

But this construction of threat by presidential Word did not stop there. The televised address of 16 March 1986, made to justify the illegal aid to the Nicaraguan Contras, synthesized six years of presidential rhetoric:

Will we permit the Soviet Union to put a second Cuba, a second Libya, right on the doorstep of the United States? Fidel Castro […], Arafat, Gadaffi and [the ayatollahs] have made their decision to support the Communists. […] Nicaragua, a Soviet ally on the American mainland […] Using Nicaragua as a base, [a command post] for international terror […] Gathered in Nicaragua [already] are [all the elements of international terror from the PLO and Italy's Red Brigade [to Colonel Gadaffi]. [Nicaragua is a threat] [...] to its democratic neighbours in Central America [...] but also for Colombia, Brazil, Ecuador, Chile, Argentina, Uruguay and the Dominican Republic [...] Established there, the USSR will be in a position to threaten the Panama Canal [...] and, ultimately, move against Mexico. Should that happen desperate Latin peoples by the millions would begin fleeing north into the cities of the southern United States.

In this astonishing speech, the president indulged in a syncretism of all strategic forms of threat, presenting them as much as forms of evil which were gathering and on the point of laying siege to, if not swamping, the United States under their weight.

This extraordinary imaginary assembly, worthy of a James Bond or a Fu Manchu film and convened by Ronald Reagan's speech, was united by the principle of a Soviet–Communist–terrorist conspiracy. The president created in the mind of those who heard it the image of a meeting room where the leading names in world terror were present under the authority of the supreme Soviet and plotting America's downfall. He gave an extraordinary relief to the idea that America was surrounded by the modern forms of evil. The social dimension added to this vision of political and strategic threat, imperilling the fabric of American society with the risk of an exodus of millions of poor, non-white, Catholic people, which would stretch the country's social tissue to the limit by saturating its *melting pot* potential. Reagan portrayed the United States as victims of an enormous encirclement manoeuvre and a geopolitical and strategic invasion.

This world vision, which became dominant in the American strategic debate, required a counter-strategy, an offensive, as much to counter the enemy as to give Americans back their sense of 'manifest Destiny'.

Cinema is intertwined with this project. While the presidency defined the threat, Hollywood put into images and defined its thought processes. This effort took shape in the great reconciliation of the national security system, Hollywood and public opinion when John Milius was filming *Red Dawn* in 1984. It was the first large-scale 'Reagan' film that unambiguously identified the Soviet Union as the principal strategic threat. One winter morning, the Soviets and the Cubans launch a surprise attack. Tens of thousand of paratroopers land in American towns and capture them. A group of college students from a small mid-West town go underground while the Red Army establishes itself in the United States. The Soviets begin a reign of terror by repression, encouraging informing and sending heads of households to the gulags. This Stalinist new order is fought by the resistance, who, at the cost of numerous sacrifices, learn Guerilla warfare and suffering, and recapture the town, whilst the rest of the country becomes the subject of a fierce Guerilla fight-back.

This strange, highly complex film, despite its slightly elementary beginnings, shows American youth, 'softened' by consumer society, thrown into a partic-ularly hostile winter environment, and end up as a group of pioneers at the vanguard of reconquering the Frontier.

*Red Dawn* takes up again this fundamental theme: young rebels (trained by a former special forces soldier who symbolizes the renewal of the 'social contract' between the defence forces and society) fight to reclaim their town and reappropriate their identity as the colonists American heirs. Through the moving image, John Milius's film revealed the implicit Nature of the spiritual dimension of American feelings about threat; Americans feeling constantly challenged by the transcendence that has chosen them, armed and coura-geous response to threat is one of the essential forms of reviving this new Alliance, of which the Dictates of Law are not written but implicit. This was implicit in all of Reagan's rhetoric and the films it inspired.

The theme of invasion, which was no longer colonizing but subversive, is reprised in Joseph Zito's *Invasion USA* (1985), starring Chuck Norris. This film shows Soviet and Cuban commandos landing in America and spreading out across the country, engaging in savage terrorism and forcing the president to declare martial law. In the film's key scene, a lorry stops in the midst of a middle-class industrial suburb. The terrorist chief gets out and begins firing a bazooka maniacally at the houses, causing death, terror and destruction.

The film illustrates American society's deep fear of subversion, who see terrorism as brutally transforming daily life into a battlefield, with neither transition nor preparation nor the possibility for adaptation. Terrorism is in this way experienced as ontologically diabolic – the etymology of which effectively comes from the Greek *diabolos*, that which divides and destroys unity in favour of confusion. Terrorism is the upsurge of murderous, arbitrary violence from outside to in, striking the very heart of the social fabric.

The process of demonizing terrorists is also accentuated by the obvious 'SS-type' Soviet terror chief. Since 1945, the figure of the Nazi has become the modern symbol of evil, that of the destruction of humanity by fanatics whose abhorrent doctrine of the superiority of one race over others replaced all affect.

As the sociologist Denis Duclos shows in *Le Complexe du loup-garou: la fascination de la violence dans la civilisation américaine*,[1] American society's morbid fascination for the image of the SS is that similar to that of the *berserker*, the 'mad warrior', for insatiable murderous violence, who embodies both the other side of the social and the threat of fiercely proud brute force triumphing over civilization.

We have to bear in mind that these movies are not propaganda films: they were not ordered by the White House nor by the Pentagon with the aim of educating the masses. They coincided with the advent of an ideological trend, the roots of which are buried in the historic, ideological, political and mythological origins of the United States. Like American society as a whole, these roots contain the strategic preoccupations of their time, and interpret them according to their frameworks of meaning and representation.

## Real Offensive, Film Offensive

But if the Soviet threat was perceived as an offensive, the virtual history proposed by Hollywood rejoined the present and dreamed up an offensive against the 'Reds', that could only take place in the ideal dimension of images, reality being the place of nuclear deterrent and symmetrical relations of power.

The offensive took place both in the USSR, Gorbachev's policy of openness being interpreted as a weakness, and in Afghanistan, 'Russia's Vietnam', a place where Soviet power was involved in a destructive war which robbed it of legitimacy, as much at home as in the sphere of international public opinion.

In Sylvester Stallone's *Rocky IV* (1985), the eponymous hero goes to Moscow to fight the Soviet champion. He knocks him out after a titanic battle under the gaze of members of the supreme Soviet. Rocky, bloodied and triumphant, drapes himself in the Stars and Stripes. Boxing becomes both a symbolic and physical confrontation of the two systems who produced the fighters.

Stallone's film projects the spectacle of combat and definitive victory over the enemy at the time when, in reality, Mikhail Gorbachev was leading the USSR out of the Soviet regime. And American cinema seized on this development not by shedding light on Glasnost but by the vision of Soviet disintegration alongside the triumphant achievement of American Destiny.

In 1988, Walter Hill's *Red Heat*, starring Arnold Schwarzenegger and James Belushi, heightened this trend. The film follows the adventures of a Moscow police officer (Arnold Schwarzenegger) who pursues a Georgian drug trafficker from the Russian capital to Chicago. The trafficker's aim is to set up an international drugs network with a black gang in the mid-West city. The Muscovite works with a disaffected local police officer but their partnership shows to what extent the foundations of Soviet society and power are shaking, whilst American society is managing to come to terms with its democratic tendency to disorder. At the same time, the film played a part in reworking the Russian threat, which was becoming international drug trafficking and the rise in power of what no-one had yet called the 'Russian mafia'.

National security cinema's new insistence on the separatist movements in train in the Soviet Union was heightened with Kevin Reynolds' *The Beast*

(1988). Here, survivors from a village where the Soviets have committed a massacre pursue a Russian tank. One of the crew members, a political science student, is so plagued with doubts about the operation that the tank commander, a former child-soldier at Stalingrad, abandons him to the Afghans. They spare the student after he asks for traditional Afghan hospitality. He then helps them repair their rocket launchers and tracks down the tank, which is eventually destroyed. Picked up by a Russian helicopter, the student realizes that he can no longer adhere to the system from which he comes.

This poignant film depicts the political, ideological, strategic and human failure of the Soviet experience. It is a clear metaphor for the breakdown of a military machine that was considered a threat to the immense forces of NATO and the United States. The film takes the image of the Soviet army, shows it worn down by the military equivalent of civil war, in-fighting, and defeated from without. The fiction of the defeat was monopolized by the American system, who put it on screen, the essential vehicle of American influence on the world stage of representations and ideas.

This imagined strategic defeat of the Soviet Union is reprised in *Rambo III*, again in 1988. This time, Rambo will save his colonel and mentor, who has been captured during a covert American support operation for the Afghan mujahadeen. With their help, Rambo infiltrates a Soviet stronghold in the heart of the mountains, frees his colonel, destroys an elite commando unit, kills the vile, SS-like major and leads the mujahadeen's charge against the remaining Soviet troops. Then, abruptly, he leaves, explaining to the child-soldier he has saved that 'this is not [his] war'. Furthermore, it is in exactly this way that American support for the mujahadeen would operate in 1990, leaving the battlefield to the Afghan extremists they have trained.

This film illustrates what was implicit and explicit in Weinberger's doctrine of 'horizontal escalation', which introduced the idea of direct or indirect conventional American reprisals wherever the Soviets were operating in the world. This doctrine involved at the same time an offensive foreign policy, which brought the confrontation between the Soviet and American hegemonies to a global level, and the processes of constructing and increasing the Soviet threat for internal political use.

In this respect, the doctrinaire thinking of the national security system was particularly effective. As Edgar Morin demonstrates in his sociology of the life of ideas, the doctrine in effect 'rejects questioning. [...] It is intrinsically irrefutable. It only selects the elements or events that conform to it; it filters them out carefully [...] and only retains from them what can be easily assimilated. The doctrine is immune to outside attacks'.[2] America's revival of the Soviet threat through discourse and cinema has thus no connection with the real state of international power relations. Above all, it involved the production of a discursive and conceptualized mechanism at the national level, the aim of which was to justify the expansion of American strategic power in the name of US security. While, in reality, the implosion process in the Soviet Union was well advanced, the hawks in the Reagan administration and conservative ideologues like Caspar Weinberger, Willam Casey, Richard Perle, Frank Gaffney or Paul Wolfowitz worked on magnifying the 'Red menace', which gave meaning to their own tragic vision of the world as a place of war against evil.

But as the United States are a large, democratic civilization, power does not exist without a counter-balance. This political reality was found again at the level of its symbolization in the sphere of images and ideas of American society. Dominant strategic thinking and representations were then questioned, and in this way supplemented, by the films of Oliver Stone, *Salvador* (1986) and *Platoon* (1986).

The ambiguous *Salvador* follows a down-at-heel, left-wing American journalist. A gifted drop-out, he denounces the collusion of the CIA with extreme right-wing forces in the name of the fight against Communism. The film follows the development of a Marxist-inspired peasant resistance movement at the same time. This movement starts a rebellion, which is bloodily put down by the American-armed right-wing government. During the key scene of the film – the battle to capture the town – the revolutionaries execute their soldier-prisoners and the journalist shouts at them: 'You have become like them!' as if it was the main issue. In this way, he blurs the distinction between Indian peasants, who revolt to avoid being killed, and genocidal soldiers. Then, during the terrifying war and repression scene that follows, all attention is focused on the risks run by two journalists.

Oliver Stone's film does not in fact criticize American political and military interventions in Latin America *per se*, but the way in which they are carried out. His aim above all is to denounce the practice of international coercion by the politically-unregulated projection of American military strength in Latin America; the atrocities committed against the El Salvadorian population were above all a pretext to make 'good impressions'. He thus denounces not the principle of intervention nor the geopolitical influence that underlies it, but its unlawfulness when it is not controlled, something which goes against the republican principles of the founding fathers.

In this way, Oliver Stone was part of the strategic debate by repeating that, from the American point of view, victory against the Soviet threat had also to adhere to precise ethical and legalist principles, for fear of seeing national security activities give rise to tyranny, against which the entire American political tradition was founded. The portrayal of Salvador's Destiny essentially supports the idealistic aim that remains anchored to the very unilateral, republican and hawkish world of strategy at this time.

Following the success of *Salvador*, Oliver Stone was able to film *Platoon*, with Charlie Sheen. The film follows a young volunteer soldier who joins an Army squadron ('Hey, guys. A crusader, we've got a crusader among us,' a black conscript guffaws). The platoon, led by a brute who gets rid of a more humanistic officer, the platoon burns down a village, *but* the inhabitants are led away kindly, children are carried by soldiers, and those who are about to rape a peasant woman are severely admonished. During the final attack on the camp, the Vietcong are only briefly glimpsed, like interchangeable shadows, the actual combat pits the brute against the idealistic, white-skinned conscript. The true battle is thus that which takes place inside the individual and collective American soul: the deployment of American forces in Vietnam is interpreted as a spiritual test. The fight against protean Communism is presented as a perfectly viable and valid ideal that is not open to criticism; but its methods are crucial. The soldier is supposed to fight for his ideal by respecting American democratic, ethical and spiritual values. If he abandons them because of war, like the brute, he runs the risk of losing his soul, and also his life.

On the other hand, the very legitimacy of the Vietnam War is not called into question. In this way, *Platoon* complements rather than goes against the wave of films that 'put the finishing touches to' the history of the war by highlighting the use of maximum, but purifying and regenerative, violence. The film itself appeals to an ethically-controlled military and strategic violence so America's ethical and ideological foundations are not put in danger. What becomes of those societies who are the theatres of political and ethical conflict peculiar to the American strategic system is only touched upon.

These films create an image of the Cold War and the indirect confrontations between these two blocs in the developing world in a manner similar to so many just American wars. They take part in the creation of a virtual history which was beginning to compete with the traumatised strategic memory in order to start the healing process and the nation's re-identification with its national security system.

## A New Strategic Legitimacy: Space Power

Another major element of dissociation between the strategic system and the American population comes from the paradox of nuclear strategy, which guarantees death as much for the enemy as those it is protecting. The issue became even more acute at the start of the 1980s, which was marked by a peak in the Reagan administration's anti-Soviet hostility. The increase in military budgets to boost the size America's nuclear arsenal and the European missiles crisis engendered anti-nuclear fervour of an unprecedented size in the history of political opposition in America.

This massive opposition came from diverse groups centred around the concept of *nuclear freeze*, who demanded a freeze on nuclear proliferation and testing. In a rare occurrence for the United States, millions of people were involved, from the political left and the right, democrats and conservatives, all faiths and none. The movement was of such a size that 500,000 people gathered in Central Park in New York in 1982 and its political expression forced senators to vote on the matter. The motion in favour of the freeze was defeated by just two votes. It should be noted that the *nuclear freeze* movement never challenged the Soviet threat in the slightest but considered nuclear weapons as a whole as much more significant.

Congress listened closely to this movement because of its national character and also because of the technological and strategic deficit that resulted from manufacturing the MX cruise missile and the 'doctrinarial disorder' it caused. The delicate 'terror balance' between the two superpowers rested on a precise accounting of weapons acquisitions operations which acted as a symbolic equivalent to the suspended war between them.

The appearance of the sophisticated MX missile was destabilizing insofar as it was never assigned a precise function such as strikes against troops, urban areas, logistics or resources. What is more, there was a problem knowing where to stockpile them. Strategic Command, useless in charge of nuclear weapons, recommended the construction of underground passages in the Mid-west, measuring tens, if not hundreds of kilometres in length, which would link the silos between which the missiles could be moved by rail. Military strategists considered that this could lead the Soviets to launch many nuclear warheads and missiles at false targets. When the senators and representatives of these states discovered the plans, the consequences of which would be clear to their electorate, they joined and spread the *nuclear freeze* idea.

The public's massive rejection of nuclear strategy caused great tension between the national security system and the cinema industry. While films that 'perfected' the Vietnam War abounded, recreating the positive link between society and the defence forces, a series of important films massively attacked the legitimacy and the hegemony of the nuclear option.

In 1983, David Cronenberg filmed *Dead Zone*, based on the Stephen King novel of the same name, with Christopher Walken. It follows the story of John Smith, an unassuming literature professor, who, after being in a coma, finds himself able to predict the future of people with whom he has shaken hands. He shakes the hand of a Midwestern political rabble-rouser who is campaigning for election to Congress. He sees him as the president and pressing THE red button, thus triggering off the first nuclear strike and proclaiming: 'I have to do it to fulfil my Destiny and that of the United States ... The missiles are launched! Hallelujah! Hallelujah!' After much thought, John decides to kill the politician. The attack fails after his intended target hides behind a baby. Shot by the politician's bodyguards, John has a final vision, that of a politician firing a bullet into his head after seeing his career ruined by the publication of photos revealing his cowardice.

This sobering and impressive film clearly associates the president's nuclear power with a potential for destruction. The nuclear option having taken root in an extremely short space of time in Information Technology and ballistics terms, it makes any political democratic mediation impossible; getting rid of nuclear weapons is thus abandoned to the whims of people who cannot be controlled. This film synthesises the questioning of what presidential power has become. Inherited from the founding fathers it has been perverted by a strategic capacity which removes it from the basic counter-balances of the republic and American democracy.

Cinema makes the legitimacy of strategic nuclear power obsolete and this takes a qualified leap in 1984 with James Cameron's *Terminator*, starring Arnold Schwarzenegger. After the Pentagon mainframe sparks nuclear war in 1997 to destroy humankind, America becomes the battlefield for a war between the survivors and machines. A fantastic warlord helps the machines secure victory. The machines thus send a robot disguised as a human to Los Angeles in order to kill the woman who will become the mother of the resistance chief before he is born. She in turn is protected by a human soldier sent from the future.

This dark film describes a human world full of the shadows of Destiny, where military technology is instrumental. Nuclear technology and its mechanisms constitute a threat in themselves, the ruthless adversary of humanity preparing to launch a 'biocide'. While technology in American society is viewed as the preferred means of developing the world to create a dreamed-of utopia, because of nuclear technology, it becomes the nightmare of inhuman forces whose work is done by negating human existence.

In this context, the questioning of nuclear technology suddenly took on a radically new dimension by adopting the position of its most militant spokesman, President Reagan. It is not a case of simple political opportunism. On the contrary, instead of winning over the anti-nuclear movement politically, because of the strong beliefs peculiar to his religious mentality, Ronald Reagan used the issue as an opportunity to declare his long-held aversion to nuclear weapons that he considered as instruments of the devil. His national security adviser, Robert MacFarlane, recalled that the president said to him: 'You know, I just hope that we will be able to get rid of these things, and be in a position to protect Americans from the scourge of annihilation.' Ronald Reagan was convinced that the United States was effectively heading straight for Armageddon, the final battle between Good and Evil. 'I tell you, that will happen, he [Reagan] said, go back to the Scriptures!'[3] The association of the anti-nuclear context and Ronald Reagan's convictions, which, at the same time, are his own and that of the collective mentality, led him to propose the Strategic Defense Initiative (SDI), an anti-missile space shield which would be made up of a group of satellites equipped with laser cannons designed to shoot down missiles heading for American soil in the event of a Soviet first strike.

The concept was labelled *Star Wars* from the day after his speech. Beyond this detail, there was nothing random about this nickname: it has a deep significance. The president, by the simple power of his words, managed to extricate the United States from the inherent illegitimacy of the nuclear deterrent and to monopolize it and any possible offensive to the Soviets, while giving himself the monopoly of noble defence.

This play on the representations and symbols which prevailed in the interpretation of international power distributions is supported by the mythology and the theological and spiritual discourse of George Lucas's *Star Wars* trilogy. The first film was shot in 1977. It relates the conflict between the 'rebel forces', who want to re-establish the galactic Republic, which used to be guarded by mystic Jedi warriors, against the Empire, which reigns with terror through stormtroopers, combat star fleets and especially its ultimate weapon, the Death Star, an enormous combat vessel whose canon is a weapon of mass destruction capable of blowing up entire planets. The Empire is led by two masters from the 'dark side of the Force', Darth Vador, a corrupted former Jedi knight, and his master, the Emperor. A young firebrand, Luke Skywalker, two robots, a bootlegger, and a former Jedi knight manage to free a former rebel leader from the Death Star who knows its weak point. The rebels then launch an attack with a fleet of small spacecraft, the last of which manages to blow up the Death Star.

This film begins a process of reversal about representations of strategic power. The ability to totally destroy a planet, which is clearly associated with the 'dark side', evil, the arbitrary Nature of tyranny, and guilty of a veritable 'Hiroshima in space', is set against the power of lasers. From *Star Wars* onwards, the laser represents the strategic dream of a discriminating, clean and mobile weapon, the mastery of which guarantees as much operational superiority as the capacity for deterrent. In addition, the film invents a new weapon: the light sabre, which is of great precision when well-handled and which requires exceptional clarity of spirit. The light sabre is the symbol of spiritual nobility, of the superiority of spirit over matter, the pre-eminence of the mystical over the political. It is the heir to the entire symbolic tradition of the sword, which ensures the connection between the 'king of justice', the spiritual forces it incarnates and the country that must be defended in times of war.

If the laser cannon associates the capacity for domination in space with the capacity for attrition and repression, the light sabre combines the exercise of power with the exercise of wisdom as the final end product of policy. Whoever possesses strategic superiority must be in a position to detach himself and to govern with wisdom, or risk passing over to the dark side of the Force. Politically, the rebels are also always legitimate, because they fight oppression from a defensive position when faced with the Empire's offensive mechanisms and starting point.

The prodigious success of this film and the two episodes that followed resulted in a context of ideas and images which provided Ronald Reagan with a point of reference. The ideas, symbols and images which cut across the film were found again in his speech of 23 March 1983, announcing the start of a massive SDI research and development programme.

> I know that this is a formidable technical task, one that may not be accomplished before the end of this century [...] But isn't it worth every investment necessary to free the world from the threat of nuclear war? [...] I call upon the scientific community in our country, those who gave us nuclear weapons, to turn their great talents now to the cause of mankind and world peace, to give us the means of rendering these nuclear weapons impotent and obsolete.

Several days later, he also declared:

> The Strategic Defense Initiative has been labelled Star Wars but it isn't about war. It's about peace. It isn't about retaliation. It's about prevention. It isn't about fear. It's about hope. And in that struggle, if you'll pardon my stealing a film line, the Force is with us.

In the series of speeches through which he brought to life the fiction of SDI as strategic reality, Ronald Reagan proposed going beyond the nuclear and ballistic model to that of space and laser power, by subscribing to the legitimizing and archetypal images created by the film, to the point of integrating them into political rhetoric. This style gave further force to the distinction between America's new definition of power, legitimacy and security and the 'evil empire'.

This division in the strategic debate between a nuclear pole, that is losing its legitimacy, and a 'rejustifying' pole, integrated into the activities of militarizing space and new technology, was transposed with great faith in film productions that encapsulate the SDI proposition.

The question of nuclear war crystallized such a collective aversion, that for the first time, Hollywood and a private television station collaborated in the production of a large-scale film for television. The first two episodes would be shown initially on US television, before transferring to American and European cinemas. *The Day After* (1983), by Nicholas Meyer with James Coburn, chronicles the disintegration of American society after a medium intensity nuclear strike.

The story alternates between the point of view of a surgeon, who takes charge of his hospital but whose resources are rapidly used up by the sick, burned and injured, and that of a farmer who is more successful in trying to keep his family together and alive. At the end of the film, the army kills people who have stolen drinking water and shoot at the hungry crowds, while farmers die slowly from radiation and two old people cry over the ashes of what was their family home.

*Testament* (1984) is more sobering still and possibly more terrifying. It follows the slow and quiet death throes of a handful of Midwest farmers. The film is punctuated by the successive burials of different members of the same family and finishes with the lonely figure of a mother burying her youngest child. The 'testament' is that of the death of society, useless family, life and hope; it will not benefit anyone. In these two films, nuclear technology is identified with an apocalypse from which there is no hope of resurrection. This cinema of despair stands in contrast to the Jedi knights.

*The Empire Strikes Back* (1980) and the *Return of the Jedi* (1983) follow the initiation of Luke Skywalker as a Jedi knight and the preparation of rebel and imperial fighters for a decisive battle. We see the confrontation of imperial fighters in large battles in space and on land, yet it is secondary to the fight between Luke and the emperor, who tries to convert him to the dark side of the Force. The technological and strategic confrontation between the two sets of troops depends on the result of this fight. The victory of the Jedi, who refuses to go over to the side of hate, at the same time saves his father, the galactic Republic and the idea of the future being a time of hope. The political and strategic message is the alliance of democracy and spirituality for a measured use of technology in war.

These films would largely contribute their popular and symbolic pertinence to Ronald Reagan's proposal for SDI. By showing the reconstitution of threat and the legitimacy to which the natural security elite aspires, they prepared the public through their catharsis and powerful images to be receptive to the strategic proposition of a 'just' militarization of space.

In this dynamic, cinema, although free from any preoccupation with propaganda, provided the new political and strategic language and became an important psychological technique, adding strategies of political discourse to their work by spreading to the nation and international community, the standards which would lead the American public to view the militarization of space as a political, religious and strategic investment, which is both profoundly beneficial and legitimate.

The conviction is then strongly implanted at all levels of 'grand strategy', as it is in society, that the nuclear deterrent was obsolete and that the embattled Soviet Union will resolve to move away from the rationale of reciprocal threat with the United States, which will speed up its disintegration. The SDI project, which benefitted from this change in strategic opinion, now became the most authentic science fiction at this time.

This international reorganization affected the very heart of the US national security system's methods of representation. In effect, representing the Soviet Union and the Communist ideology as strategic threats was the basis for the complex political manoeuvring which ended in its institutional creation between 1945 and 1947. The turnaround instigated by Mikail Gorbachev from 1985 and the acceleration of the thawing of US–Soviet relations caused the threat to disappear. The rationale behind US policies towards the diplomatic thawing, from the increase in openness under the Gorbachev regime and the bilateral decision to reduce the number of nuclear weapons, ended in an astonishing synthesis: that of the transformation of the Soviet threat into a peace process between the two superpowers.

## The Virtualization of the USSR

The severely weakened Soviet Union begun to show a willingness to cooperate with Washington. The move from the production of threat to the production of cooperation posed a sizeable problem for the Americans in terms of national security: who was the enemy now?

This strategic transmutation is the subject of John McTiernan's 1990 film, *The Hunt for Red October*, starring Alec Baldwin and Sean Connery. A Soviet submarine commander is supposed to take the pride of the Soviet fleet, the stealthy, nuclear missile-equipped Red October, out on manoeuvres. Once at sea, the commander kills the vessel's political officer and secretly changes the instructions for the mission: Red October then heads for the United States. Panicked by this defection, the Soviets ask for American help in finding and sinking the submarine, on the grounds that the commander has gone mad and that he is liable to launch his missiles against the United States. A young CIA analyst and specialist in maritime strategy, Jack Ryan, puts forward the theory that it is a defection: Red October wants to seek refuge in the United States. What follows is a game of cat and mouse between American and Soviet submarines and warships, during which Jack Ryan is smuggled on board Red October, whose officers have ordered the crew off in the middle of the ocean, and asked for political asylum. After escaping an attempt by a Soviet submarine to sink it, Red October arrives at Nantucket, and Jack Ryan welcomes the Russian commandant with the follow: 'Welcome to the land of the free, commander!'

This film manages to dismantle the idea of the Soviet Union as a threat by the spectacle of a defection from that ultimate guarantee of deterrence, the submarine fleet, submarines being the only vessels carrying nuclear weapons to be truly invincible because they are virtually undetectable. The film's strategic problem is that of surrendering this ultimate bulwark of the Soviet Union to the Americans, incapacitating the political apparatus it is supposed to be defending as a result.

On the other hand, this 'transfer of technology' only increases American technological and military potential and heralds the dissemination of the 'land of the free' ideology across the world, while US military power spreads itself easily and permanently on the seas. This film thus actively played a part in the virtualization of the USSR as its defence systems (whether real, in the case of the missiles, or imaginary, as in the film) underwent drastic reductions because of the attraction exerted by the idea of peace with America. For the Soviets, this was equally synonymous with the possibility of living in peace *in* America, an ideal to substitute for the dictatorship of the proletariat. The film effectively shows the Russians all at sea and ending up finding safe harbour.

From reading the script, this film's importance was not lost on the US Navy. Compared to the Army and the Air Force, the film made the Navy out to be the only really strategic force of the Cold War because it was the only one to be in permanent contact with the enemy by crossing the lines of navigation and the incessant game of deadly hide-and-seek between the submarines of both fleets. This led to mobilization on a rarely-seen scale: the Navy opened up the famous Norfolk naval yards to the film crew and loaned an aircraft carrier, helicopters and several warships, all under a chain of command whose purpose was to manoeuvre them to the dictates of the script in the middle of an unremittingly rough Atlantic Ocean. The Navy demonstrated itself publicly as the armed service where heroism is constant when faced with Nature and the enemy. The cooperation between the studios, the military and the political ranks, was such that the Admiral of the Atlantic fleet was played by Fred Thompson, an amateur actor and more particularly a Republican senator, whose high-standing and charisma suits the film's demands its series of messages. (Fred Thompson would later play the New York airport director taken hostage in 1990 in *Die Hard 2*, and the American president's cabinet chief in the 1993 film by Wolfgang Petersen, *In the Line of Fire*, while remaining a permanent Republican leading light in Congress.)

The Reagan years are therefore those where, by means of images about strategy, the United States established itself in the role of schoolmaster – making pronouncements about the absolutes of good, evil and the law – against the arbitrary embodied in the Soviet threat. But the disappearance of the Soviet threat, by bringing about the need to find and create new threats, would in fact cause a crisis of adjustment between cinema and strategy.

# 4

# NEW THREATS, 1990–1994

The problem at the end of the Cold War was the disappearance of the Soviet threat and consequently that of the sense of legitimacy about the existence and size of the American national security system. However, the convergence and synergy of cinema and strategy provided those in charge of the latter with a language that facilitated the production of new representations of threat.

## Script or Political Language?

The use of these new devices by the national security elite thus took place at the time when the American strategic system was in search of new threats and where Saddam Hussein, the faithful and well-supported ally of the United States, invaded Kuwait, after warning the American ambassador to Baghdad and not having received any clear response from the State Department nor from the White House.

President George Bush decided then, with the agreement of the oil-producing Saudi monarchy, to deploy American troops on its soil and to create an international coalition to ensure the security of the Saudi allies. From October 1990, the White House took the initiative to increase the number of troops from 250,000 to 500,000 men in the Gulf, so as to allow, eventually, the launch of an offensive against the Iraqi army in Kuwait. In order to do this, he had to obtain the agreement of Congress who control the purse strings for war.

The debate that ensued in Congress between moderates and hawks was extremely lively (each being equally spread between Democrats and Republicans) and centred on the legitimacy of an intervention in Iraq. To carry the motion, the hawks constructed a rhetorical device which defined Iraq as a new threat and thus justified the recourse to massive force.

This move took place during the hearings of Congress between October and November 1990 by the Senate Commission on Armed Forces. The hawks aim to transform Saddam Hussein and Iraq into a pressing target for attack was backed with persuasive methods directly inspired by national security cinema. The phenomenon is particularly apparent during speeches by Henry

Kissinger and Richard Perle. Henry Kissinger, a 'realist' in favour of an offensive against Iraq, declares:

> To abandon Kuwait to Iraq [...] will lead sooner or later, and I think sooner rather than later, to a very high risk of conflicts between moderate Arab nations and extremist nations, as well as to the near certainty of an Arab-Israeli conflict in which this time there would be a very strong possibility of the use of nuclear weapons....[1]

This strange declaration is presented in the rational guise of a cold and dispassionate analysis made by a former university academic, national security adviser to Richard Nixon and very high-ranking diplomat, whilst it is really about a fictitious situation, described 'like in the movies'.

In effect, there is no Iraqi–Israeli border nor 'extremist' or 'moderate' nations. Israel is the only State in the region to have nuclear weapons. On the other hand, Henry Kissinger's speech works around the combination of national security issues, the strategic alliance with Israel, relations with Arab countries and the question of nuclear proliferation, and has as its aim the creation of dramatic imagery. The Arab–Israeli–American war can only exist in the American mental universe of strategic make-believe. Far from rational analysis, Henry Kissinger is basically addressing here the culpability and fascination of Americans, who are already caught up in a culture of image and cinema drama, with Israel and with the recall of nuclear fear.

This process was reprised by another hawk, Richard Perle, a former deputy secretary of Defense to Ronald Reagan and close to the Bush administration. He was one of the main political actors chosen to 'sell' SDI to the Pentagon between 1983 and 1988. Having expended great energy to this through more or less secret networks, he established himself as an implacable technician and polemicist. He acquired the nickname 'Prince of Darkness'. Following the Reagan administration, he joined the board of the American Enterprise Institute, an ultra-conservative lobby group to the right of the Republican party (it should be noted that since 2000, Richard Perle has led the very influential Defense Policy Board; he is a key player in the current creation of US unilateral and neo-conservative strategy).

This surprising figure, ideologically to the right of Henry Kissinger, engages in a similar script-like anticipation. After comparing Saddam Hussein to Hitler, an effective method of justifying armed intervention, he goes on:

> No-one can maintain with certainty how Saddam Hussein will use his military power and influence in the Gulf. That he will look to destroy the leaders of other Gulf States there is no doubt but where will he stop? No

oil for Western fleets in the Mediterranean? No oil for countries refusing to give him the necessary technology to complete his acquisition of nuclear weapons? No oil produced in collaboration with American producers? No oil for countries who extradite terrorists?… It is much more likely that he will support international terrorism and Holy War while installing many little Saddams across the world![2]

This portrait of Saddam Hussein, astounding if we consider that months earlier he was still one of the United States preferred allies in the Middle East, notably for having beaten Ayatollah Khomenei's Iran, fits in to a cinematic genealogy of threat.

Richard Perle makes Saddam Hussein out to be the successor not only to Hitler and Stalin, but also, even especially, to the masters of strategic blackmail present exclusively in national security cinema and literature. He highlighted the dimension of effective geopolitical blackmail which actually did not exist with the USSR. His speech is above all an idea of the world to come dominated by the crisis of a lethal spiral of violence that only American power is capable of wiping out. This Machiavellian Saddam described by Richard Perle mirrors a previous incarnation, the head of Spectre. This international criminal organisation, fought regularly by James Bond since *From Russia With Love* in 1963, decides in *Thunderball* (1965) to resort to nuclear blackmail with the bombs they have stolen; Spectre returns to the attack the democracy and security of NATO and the United States in 1967 in *You Only Live Twice, Diamonds Are Forever* in 1971 and in 1983 in *Never Say Never Again*. Using blackmail by weapons of mass destruction is a constant with Spectre: the organisation is evidently driven by the taste for evil and madness beyond vulgar materialistic interests.

In other respects, the reference in the speech to 'Arab-Islamist' terrorism does not relate at that time to any event on American soil, but only to films produced on the subject when Ronald Reagan was president, such as *Delta Force* (1985), in which Chuck Norris leads an elite Army unit and wipes out a terrorist network in Beirut. In fact, the classic film figure stuck onto the 'eastern' face of Saddam Hussein is that of a key figure in cinema entertainment, the diabolic Dr Fu Manchu, who, between 1905 and the arrival of talkies, signified the 'yellow peril' and was the forerunner of national security cinema.

What we can describe as the 'passion for the worst' is evident in the production of national security film scenarios which invoke the risk of major catastrophe in order to make heroes of secret agents, commandos and elite police officers, whilst effectively, they are not characters with which we can readily associate. On the other hand, they become icons in the alternative world of film and the Republican hawks reinvest this passion for the worst in political speeches at the time when the national security system was looking to use the crisis in the Gulf as an opportunity to create a new threat.

What was implicit in the discourse of grand strategy thus combined cinematic representations of 'super-criminality' with those of 'eastern tyranny'. These two speakers aims were thus to trigger off a 'passion for the worst' and to allay public fears not by witnessing the defeat of threatening figure but by the reality of war presented as an assignment for James Bond, Rambo, Bruce Willis or Arnold Schwarzenegger.

In associating the possibility of the proliferation of terrorism with that of nuclear military proliferation from the single diabolic figure of Saddam Hussein, Richard Perle elevates him to the level of 'Master of Darkness', to a kind of Middle Eastern Darth Vader. In addition, he raises once again the repressed horror of Hiroshima and Nagasaki actualized in cinema since the 1950s. To use Pierre Clastres expression, he is engaging in a 'grand talking',[3] transmuting the factual, geopolitical reality into scenarios of national security films.

This rhetorical exercise led by the hawks was effective, moreover, because conjuring up the imaginary and images of threat left the moderates in an awkward position through the impossibility of declaring with absolute certainty that the threat of an oil crisis and from nuclear weapons, terrorists and Islamic extremists presented no risk at all to American society. They were trapped by the belief in the possible and the worst in which the hawks had set out the strategic debate and, finding themselves incapable of denouncing the unrealistic Nature of national security scenarios developed in the name of the actual security of the United States. The hawks won the vote in Congress which allowed the deployment of 250,000 extra men and the recourse to offensive force against Iraq in Kuwait.

The offensive started on 15 January 1991 with a five-week bombing campaign, followed by an extraordinary pincer movement of Army land forces in a lightning strike lasting no more than 100 hours. This remarkable *Blitzkrieg* operation eradicated the US forces traumatic memory of being stuck in Vietnam and would be eclipsed by Hollywood.

All American wars and strategic crises since 1942 have been made into films, with a reactivity in keeping with America's industrial capacity for adaptation, not only the Second World War, the Korean War, the Vietnam War and the attack on Grenada but also the recurrent crisis brought about by the existence of nuclear weapons and the upsurge in tension as with the Cuban crisis. On the other hand, for Hollywood, the Gulf War never took place, with the exception, in 1996, of *Courage Under Fire*, which uses the land offensive as a pretext for a military drama where the Iraqis are never seen, and

*Three Kings*, which came out in 1999, eight years after the war at a time when national security cinema was characterized by a great reactivity towards actual events.

This absence is deeply significant of the limits of the relationship between the national security system, the wars it fights and the cinema industry. The Gulf War, despite the twin performances firstly by the rhetoric of the hawks, then by CNN with its round-the-clock 'War in the Gulf' programme, is not perceived by American public opinion as a defence operation.

On the contrary, its offensive Nature, with recourse to coercion to compensate the crisis of the American strategic system's hegemony in the Middle East, makes it a very difficult subject to film. In effect, this political dominance is largely founded on political pressures and sales of arms and military material to all countries in the region, including Israel, Iraq and Iran, since the 1960s. The clearly offensive Nature of the Gulf War, in the name of power interests, as well as the total asymmetry of military means and will, makes it impossible to portray by creating heroes without clearly denying the reality of the situation: national security films need this reality as support.

The heroes of these films put their lives on the line in the name of their superiors, who are characterized by national security ideology, to save lives and a certain vision of the world: that of freedom and democracy as defined by American civilization. But the Gulf War is, in one obvious sense, a non-heroic operation of military adjustment of power and hegemony that it is 'forgotten' in a way to avoid starting a crisis between Washington and Hollywood.

## A Cardboard Geo-political Analysis

The penetration of language and American political argument by the make-believe of national security cinema was carried on and increased after the Gulf War at the time when the disappearance of the Soviet enemy brought about reconstitution of strategic ideologies.

The phenomenon is particularly apparent in Samuel Huntington's famous article of 1992 on the 'clash of civilizations', which was later turned into a book in 1994.[4] Samuel Huntington, a leading military sociologist and specialist in international relations at Harvard during the Cold War, believed that, after the fall of the Berlin Wall, the world would see the reconstitution of 'blocs' of both political beliefs and civilizations. For Huntington, a large western civilization (that he identifies as America and its European allies) exists which risk suffering the hostility of other blocs of civilizations in years to come, in particular from the strange invention of the 'Islamo-Confucian axis', an alliance of Islamic countries (in particular Iran) and Confucianist China who share a common hatred of 'the West' (the United States).

In fact, Samuel Huntington's stated aim is to propose a new definition of threat so as to save his country from breaking up into multiple communities whose values, he asserts, are incompatible with those of the United States. Huntington's argument, in the guise of a university thesis, is in fact a militant, even impassioned, argument that puts white, Anglo-Saxon, Protestant America in a future world subjected to the constant threat of a war between civilizations.

To give substance to his argument, he pens a scenario that could be the script for the Third World War (p. 346 French edition of 1997). He imagines that China invades Vietnam, who in turn asks for American help. The conflict evolves in China's favour after Japan has been brought in and they begin to threaten Russia, while India destroys Pakistan with nuclear weapons, triggering off the 'civilizational reflex' of a Muslim world 'united' by religion. The confrontations provoke the restarting of the conflict in Yugoslavia and Serbia attacks NATO-protected Bosnia. 'Islamic Algeria' fires a nuclear missile on Marseilles and north Africa is subjected to a series of Western nuclear strikes. The firing of nuclear weapons leads to the devastation of the 'West', Russia and China, whilst India and Indonesia become beacon states and the balance of world power 'tips towards the south'.

Samuel Huntington's scenario plays on the same imagination as that of someone watching a national security film: the actors from the international civilizations are characters created in a dramatic device where action dominates and in which the substance lies in creating suspense regardless of the realities of war and diplomacy. A straight line can be drawn from the idea of international nuclear war to national security films that portrayed it: the first, *On The Beach* (1959), and *Dr Strangelove* (1963), both end with the destruction of western civilization, and in the case of Stanley Kubrick's film, on the 'ballet' of nuclear explosions.

American readers of Huntington were among the tens of millions of television viewers who saw Nicholas Meyer's *The Day After* in 1983 with its terrifying launching of intercontinental missiles, followed by the disintegration of American society. Just after the Gulf War, James Cameron's *Terminator II* is haunted by nuclear fear and its images of war and its aftermath are among the most distressing ever shown on film.

In Huntington's text, this imagined reality is interspersed with the old American fantasy of the 'yellow peril', elegantly reworked under the auspices of the threat posed by 'Confucian civilization' and 'Chinese power'. China has never attacked the United States. The only direct military confrontation between the two took place during the Korean War and it had been started by the American decision to cross the Yalu river. The representation of China as bellicose, expansionist and anti-American dates back to the super-productions of the 1950s and 1960s: *55 Days At Peking* (1962), where Charlton Heston

ensures the safety of western expatriates in Peking during the Boxers revolt in
1905; *The Sand Pebbles* (1966), where Steve McQueen, a marine, goes up the
Yellow River opposing the anti-Chinese racism of his comrades until he is
killed by the Chinese; then, in 1967, *Battle Beneath the Earth* shows a Chinese
Popular Army plot to dig a tunnel between China and Los Angeles in order
to invade California by literally going through the sewers. The 'yellow peril'
idea is taken up again by Michael Cimino in *The Year of the Dragon* (1985)
which envisages the infiltration of American society and power by the Triads.

Samuel Huntington thus renews the definition of strategic threat by the discursive crossing of two cinematographic traditions of nuclear catastrophe and
the 'yellow peril' within what is supposed to be a factual geo-political analysis.
But this withdrawal from empirical reality, as with the Soviet Union, anchors
the threat in the sphere of a collective American mental environment which
is directly in tune with films.

Cinema's infiltration of grand strategy – from the 1980s of Ronald Reagan
to the political and strategic status of Samuel Huntington and to the level of producing strategic paradigms which can be used by politicians – was largely the
work of the conservative wing of the American national security establishment.

The national security establishment is effectively a complex group, organized into multiple networks which are ideologically united by the fear of
seeing American society weakened and falling into decline while the world
creates even more dangerous new threats. This tragic mentality, which is not
based on facts but on a perception of the world, is suited to a systematic resort
to force to get rid of any movement deemed to be dangerous.

For Hollywood, the end of the Cold War meant a marked tailing off in
making conservative movies, at least in the area of national security. It was, on
the other hand, a favourable period for liberal film makers who did not have
a tragic vision of America's relationship with the world. This ideological
divergence explains why national security films were little influenced by the
Huntington ideology between 1992 and 2000, while even that argument was
quickly making inroads into a number of military and political sectors.

On the other hand, a film like *True Lies* (1993) by James Cameron makes a
farce out of this tragic vision. This film, a remake of Claude Zidi's *La Totale*,
follows a secret agent (Arnold Schwarzenegger) belonging to a kind of 'super
CIA', who convinces his family he is a run-of-the-mill computer engineer. He
discovers that 'eastern' terrorists are hatching a plot to blow up nuclear
weapons in several American cities. The terrorists, whose pronouncements
allow them to be clearly identified as Iraqis, get into the United States with
the help of a firm specializing in the trade of Mesopotamian antiquities. Little
by little, statues, tapestries and other Babylonian and Assyrian props invade
the space, to the point where they act as the backdrop when the terrorist

leader records his message. But these antiquities are revealed to be fakes containing weapons and the terrorists are shown up as buffoons, whose modern equipment is beyond them, and as the real victims of American hegemony in the Middle East. In this way, James Cameron's film casts an original light on Huntington's proposition of the definition of threat and shows to what extent the 'civilization' definition of strategic threat has as much substance as cardboard.

On the other hand, James Cameron's choice of showing the terrorists on screen comes plainly from the new alignment being formulated by the national security establishment of *clear and present danger*, above all from terrorists and the developing world, against a backdrop of US-Russian reconciliation.

## The End of the Cold War and Terrorism

The fall of the Soviet Union in December 1991 followed the Gulf War. The uneasy peace that was established then destabilized the American national security system which needs threats to justify its existence, identity and budgets. Hollywood, on the other hand, can continue to produce films about subjects other than national security. The crisis of the strategic system appeared almost structural between 1991 and 1995 and who not helped by the political and ideological renewal that followed Bill Clinton's election to the United States presidency.

While with George Bush the national security system's political direction was guaranteed by high-ranking professionals for whom foreign policy and strategy was a virtual way of life and a way of thinking, constantly assessing the United States position in relation to the real or supposed State of the enemy's strengths, Bill Clinton was elected on a neo-isolationist platform, his favourite slogan being: 'We must think about the Middle-West before thinking about the Middle East.' Once in power, President Clinton and his team had little taste for foreign policy, even less for strategy. On the other hand, the first military setback, that of special forces in Mogadishu in 1993, was followed by a unilateral and immediate withdrawal of American troops from the United Nations forces in Somalia. International relations only interested Clinton and his team at the level of world trade; they ignored international relations and were only concerned about them when constrained and forced. In addition, Congress was taken up with the return in force of Republicans and the radical Christian right, as well as by the arrival of neo-conservatives, led by Newt Gingrich. The political agenda was then very much dominated by internal issues. The American world of strategy was thus more or less left to its own devices, hunting for threats.

From 1989 to 1990, the different centres of the national security system began publishing lists of threats corresponding to an 'imminent danger'; in no particular order, we find international terrorism, drug traffickers and refugee groups. The first two threats are subject to rapid stage management from 1991. The idea is deeply entwined with the terrorist threat and became sufficiently important at this time for the cinema to appropriate it with Phillip Noyce's adaptation of the Tom Clancy novel, *Patriot Games* (1992), starring Harrison Ford.

The film begins in London with an Irish terrorist attack on a member of the Royal Family. The attack fails because of the intervention of Jack Ryan, a CIA analyst who happens to be sightseeing in London with his family. The terrorists, from a hard-line faction of the IRA, pursue and attack him in revenge on American soil. The CIA is involved then in a first 'war against terrorism'. Using phone taps, the terrorists are tracked down to Libya where they have gone on a training exercise. There then follows a very impressive sequence: via a satellite that transmits live, infra-red images of the surprise, night-time commando operation, CIA officials follow the destruction of the camp and the massacre of the terrorists. Those who survive it later attack Jack Ryan again on American soil and once more, they are on the losing side.

This films communicates several political and strategic messages. One of the most important sequences is the moment when, after an attempt to assassinate his wife and daughter, Jack Ryan obtains a list of names of Irish terrorists from an official IRA representative who is on a fund-raising tour of the United States, after threatening to condemn the IRA at a press conference in the intensive care room where his child is being treated.

The US federal State had maintained extremely ambiguous links with Irish republicans for a long time of the pressure exerted by the Irish lobby, who were very powerful in Washington and in Congress (we will recall, for example, the Irish origins of the Kennedy family). Numerous IRA and Sinn Fein staging posts exist in American towns with large populations of Irish origin, which constitute important sources of funding, hence the political and military problems for Britain.

But, from 1992, American policy underwent a large-scale shift, implicitly accompanied and prepared by *Patriot Games*, which made the divorce official between Washington and the IRA, provided they did not revert to armed violence. In the years that followed, President Clinton's national security adviser, Anthony Lake, would be deeply involved in the negotiations between the British government, Sinn Fein and the IRA. *Patriot Games* thus heralds the reinforcement of strategic links between Great Britain and the United States. This reinforcement takes place in the scene where Jack Ryan is ennobled and becomes Lord Ryan, the embodiment of America's new identity as an empire.

The strategic message is found in the speed with which the CIA – and through it the American system – adapt to new terrorist threats, the promotion of which it effectively ensures. The updating of new combat methods also corresponds to this new definition of threat, in particular those from space, which are largely to the fore in this film.

This period of reconstitution was just as awkward for the national security system in that it was susceptible to being laid bare by the disappearance of the Soviet threat, which acted as its safeguard. This risk is the subject of Phillip Noyce's *Clear And Present Danger*, an adaptation of the Tom Clancy novel and again starring Harrison Ford.

In a fit of rage, the president of the United States orders his national security adviser to launch a secret combat operation against the Colombian Cali cartel. The adviser then asks the director of operations at the CIA to assemble an undercover team and send it to Colombia without alerting the director of the 'analysis' section who would be against the plan. At the same time, the assistant-director, Jack Ryan, is solemnly promising to the Senate Commission on the activities of the intelligence service to ban all clandestine operations. American soldiers start blowing up laboratories in the jungle and killing the drug barons but the head of security and most powerful among them, a former Cuban spy, discovers them and realises that the operation is totally illegal. With the greatest secrecy, he contacts the national security adviser and offers to regulate drug trafficking once he has seized control of the cartel. For that to happen, the American soldiers have to be handed over to the Colombian mercenaries. The presidential adviser accepts. By chance, Jack Ryan learns what is happening. He puts together a counter-operation to rescue the survivors, informs the head of the cartel of the double-dealing in progress and goes to the Senate to testify about the whole process, which will cost the president his job.

This complex film links two types of threat for American society: drug traffickers and the tyrannical potential of the American State, notably in its foreign policy. The Colombian drug producers and traffickers are presented as a commercial/military organization whose immense financial resources allow them to maintain mercenaries and security measures. It is legitimate to consider them as a threat, all the more so since they export their violence to the United States not only through drugs but also by criminality, which enrages the presidenti.

But this *clear and present danger* is not sufficient to justify the drift of the national security system of which the film provides an exhaustive list: the president makes anticonstitutional decisions, the CIA frees itself from Congressional control, troops are sent abroad without any officially-sanctioned chain of command, public funds are diverted in order to mount an illegal operation which leads to a massacre of women and children by the Navy and commandos.

In this context of American political culture, these *faux pas* are symptomatic of the tyrannical potential of the State. The film thus assumes responsibility for the mistrust towards the State, the founder of American political culture, which is characterized by the increase in counter-balances so as to avoid the emergence of a central tyrannical power.

To understand this important film, we have to put it in its correct political context. The author of the original novel, Tom Clancy, has practically become the official adaptor of catastrophic scenarios handed to him by the CIA and the Pentagon, with which he has maintained privileged links since the world-wide success of *The Hunt for Red October*. He is the second most-read American author in the world after Stephen King. His books all put forward a Republican, very much right-wing, militaristic, unilateralist and conservative point of view. He himself is, among other things, an active lobbyist for the Republican party; the garden of his house is adorned with an authentic Second World War tank. The effectiveness of his writing comes chopping up the prose into short and compelling sequences, which can be easily adapted for cinema, as well as a knowledge and deep understanding of the political games between the different people in charge of national security.

The adaptations of his novels in cinema are faithful to the narrative framework, whereas that of *Clear and Present Danger* is clearly of a Democratic and moderate inspiration, and comes to remind the public what risks the Republican power regularly has to weigh up. In effect, the film does not trouble itself recalling the Watergate scandal, which cost the Republican Nixon his presidency, making allusions in passing to Henry Kissinger – many times the *ex officio* 'dubious operations' adviser – nor to the large and a lot more recent scandal of Irangate.

In 1985, one of Ronald Reagan's national security advisers, Colonel Oliver North, had effectively organized illegal sales of American weapons via the Israeli secret service, Mossad, to Iran, who were at war with America's ally, Iraq, in order to pour the profits back to the CIA-backed Nicaraguayan contras. The scandal was such that President Reagan had to face questioning before a Senate commission of enquiry.

In fact, in this national security film, the democrats in Hollywood during Bill Clinton's presidency take part in straight fight against the increase in Republican power, while employing the prevailing strategic argument that identifies Colombian drug traffickers with strategic threats. The film itself plays the part of counter-balance against the power of the majority conservative ideology in Congress.

In this way, at a time when we see an upsurge in national security cinema between 1992 and 1994 of an attempt to renew the strategic and political problem of threat while consensus is no longer ensured by the giant threat of the Soviet Union, it is the terrorist question, more generally, that challenges the issue of societal cohesion.

# 5

# THE NEED TO FIGHT TERRORISM, 1994–2000

Terrorism is not a new subject in national security cinema. Its first, albeit rare, manifestations date back to the 1970s. It returns more often in the middle of the Reagan years, but it really makes its presence felt at the forefront of productions from the mid-1990s.

Terrorism is an extremely sensitive strategic subject for Americans because it poses the twin problem of societal subversion and cohesion inside a society which has the greatest difficulty accepting its own unity. The theme of subversion, this capacity for undermining the foundations of society, is the highly implicit sub-text of America's relationship with terrorism. The sudden appearance of this age-old American fear in recent national security cinema is explained by the sense of anguish shared by society, the military and the foreign policy and national security community when faced with a world that can no longer be explained by the Soviet threat, but which, nonetheless, could endanger the American social system.

Compared with a society like that of France, whose cohesion has been tested and which is thoroughly established in time, wrought and constructed by two thousand years of history, American society sees something terrifying in the idea of subversion experienced in a major threat, which is understood as a phenomenon capable of causing a split such that social life and all personal safety of individuals could disappear, the framework of daily life becoming a deadly trap.

The theme of terrorism established itself in the different areas of national security, as much official ones as private. The CIA created the centre for counter-terrorism whilst the National Security Agency (NSA) specializes in phone-tapping, attempting to deal with all 'sensitive' conversations. The different sectors of the American army updated the training of special forces in the fight against terrorists, while the large think tanks, the 'ideas factories', private consultancy firms who formulated the essential areas of American nuclear and spatial strategy during the Cold War, embarked upon research on terrorism.

The historic think-tank the RAND Corporation, which was founded in 1946 by the association of Lockheed and the Air Force and which produced the most important concepts during the years of nuclear deterrent in America, became a pole of research on terrorism to such an extent that the work of the department's director, Bruce Hoffman, was translated into several languages.

The strategy production industry was thus polarized around the terrorism question between the end of the 1980s and the end of the Gulf War, well before the attack on the basement of the World Trade Center in 1993. This unique event, as well as the Al-Qaida attacks against American embassies in Kenya and Tanzania in 1998, would feed the terrorist threat production industry until 2001.

## The Threat of Subversion

This repolarisation of American strategic affairs effectively involves all issues about societal cohesion, which seems, potentially, to be called into question by the disappearance of the Soviet threat and the consensus it produced. In effect, Colombian drug traffickers, terrorists and networks of all types existed well before the fall of the USSR, but the danger they posed was not established to the same level it was created in American society.

This vulnerability of the social world, increased by terrorist subversion, is the very subject of *Speed* (1994), by Jan De Bont, starring Keanu Reeves. A disgruntled former bomb disposal expert with the Los Angeles Police Department (LAPD), plants a number of devices in the city. He fits one of them to a bus, which will explode if the vehicle's speed goes below 50mph. A young police officer from an elite unit is informed and manages to get on the bus. He must then keep it moving at speed through the hellish Los Angeles traffic while defusing the bomb attached under the bus and evacuating the passengers from it.

The film revolves around showing the subversion of one of the mainstays of American daily life, that is, getting around a large city. By transforming lifts, buses and underground trains into terrorist targets, the former police officer booby-traps the city. Daily activities become potentially deadly. Terrorism then subjects the relationship with space and urban moments to the uncertain temporality of terrorist blackmail. City dwellers perpetual comings and goings require a very precise mastery of time, transport structuring individual, familial, professional and social time. When transport is disrupted, and transformed into a time of terror and deadly threat, the time for engaging in social activities is undermined, and becomes that for the production of the terrorist project. The film expresses this process by demonstrating Los Angeles no longer as a place where a working and peaceful society proliferates, busy going about its daily business, but as an ambivalent trap which needs to be escaped and which becomes both an actual and parallel space, in the midst of which terror spreads. In this way, the city, trapped in a fragile space/time continuum, splits into two, becoming simultaneously a framework of life and the space for the sudden appearance of arbitrary armed violence.

*Speed* effectively tells the story of the random extraction of a group of American citizens, the prime example of the urban civilization of Los Angeles, in order to throw them into the modern version of the Frontier, by making the city's road and motorway network the place, as hostile and dangerous as Nature was for the first colonists, for an ordeal that results in either death or a change in identity through the unleashing of violence and ingenuity against danger.

Nevertheless, fear of subversion goes right to the heart of the very concept of society by the notion of social contract, by transforming the urban space of society into a battlefield. This happened in New York in 1995 in John McTiernan's *Die Hard: With a Vengeance*, starring Bruce Willis. This film is the third in the 'John MacLane' trilogy, begun in 1988 with *Die Hard*, in which tough guy police officer John MacLane defeats would-be terrorists who have taken hostage the staff of a Japanese firm in Los Angeles in order to mask their real objective: seizing tens of millions of dollars' worth of Treasury bills stored in the firm's safe. John MacLane has to be called in again in 1990 in Renny Harlin's *Die Hard 2* to free a New York airport from extreme-right wing American mercenaries and former special forces operatives, who want to liberate a Latin American dictator who has been extradited to the United States to stand trial, even though he supported American anti-Communist policy for years. This film anticipates *Speed* by the sudden appearance of corrosive violence in the midst of a vital air transport hub which allows a connection between both the Pacific and Atlantic coasts and the world.

In the third episode in 1995, terrorist subversion brings New York to the brink of urban warfare. A series of explosions (the biggest of which is on Wall Street) is followed by claims about the fight against American imperialism. The discovery of numerous bombs, including one in Central Park and another in a high school, forces the mayor to call in the National Guard and to declare off martial law. The 'real' terrorists are in fact an elite former East German army unit: they have caused pandemonium in the city/world as a diversion, their real goal being to steal the gold reserves of the central bank of New York. They are foiled by the supercop Bruce Willis, servant of the law and guarantor of local order, in the fight against the militarization and trans-nationalization of armed criminality.

This film is supposed to be a commentary on the violence of the strategic relationship prevailing between the cohesion of urban society in the United States and the geo-political development of the world. This relationship is underlain by the transformation of criminality into terrorism which takes it beyond the level of traditional, subversive force, which is normally kept in check by police forces, to that of militarized strategic power, which requires new means of control and repression. John McTiernan's film established itself in this way as one of the voices in strategic affairs and the issue of the militarization of the United States' internal security.

The American tendency to employ military means for social control is not new but it made its presence felt at the turn of the 1980s and increased throughout the 1990s. It involved turning police, and therefore security forces into organizations armed with military equipment and with less of a police mentality than a war-like one.

This militarization process of the security forces has been particularly noticeable since the Los Angeles riots in 1992. In his sociological study of Los Angeles, *City of Quartz*, Mike Davis demonstrates how the city is seen by the LAPD as a mosaic where some neighbourhoods are peaceful whilst others are treated like war zones with officers behaving 'like an army of occupation'. In order to do this, the LAPD went through intensive militarization during the 1980s. The development of patrol tactics and strongly offensive urban control was improved by setting up on-line data-banks on delinquency and criminality, with everything coordinated by the systematic use of helicopters for patrolling, surveillance and tracking. These different interlinked devices gave the police a much-improved intrusion, control and strike capacity.

In addition, police officers underwent martial arts training, even in infantry and hand-to-hand combat techniques – including the *krav maga*, a hand-to-hand combat technique of the Israeli army. This perception of the urban space as a place of war was increased by media accounts during the riots in Los Angeles (1992 and 1998), New York (1999) and Cincinnati (April 2001).

During the Cincinnati riots, where the siege then assault on a black ghetto by the police forces was shown, Keith Fangman, the president of the Association of American Municipal Police, declared on CNN on 15 April 2001: 'Police forces have to be better trained in the escalation and de-escalation of conflicts.' These words, his vocabulary and the mentality that underpins it, come straight from the terms and concepts used in the nuclear strategy during the Cold War and which crept into operational military strategy during the Vietnam War. Furthermore, it must be remembered that numerous war veterans joined the police. Social conflicts are then expressed in terms of violent subversion and raise fears of seeing disorder reign, the peace of towns and cities giving way then to the 'war of everyone against everyone', hence the confusion of the 'whole security' ideology, which is based on that of the 'threatening whole' and justifies the militarization of security.

Cinema, in this case, makes itself an enthusiastic participant in this switch, thanks in particular to the remarkable dramatic potential offered by the militarized view of crime and security and of the 'just combat' of the latter against the subversion that threatens to break up society.

One year after winning the Vietnam War by seeing off the Soviets, Sylvester Stallone militarized the Los Angeles police against the army of crime in *Cobra*, by George Pan Cosmastos (1986). A group of serial killers is attacking the population and police force of Los Angeles. They act like an invading army driven by an ideology of sadistic anarchy and possessing a vast military arsenal. An elite police officer, codenamed Cobra, who behaves like a commando, takes them on and kills them with weapons of war. He declares that war and the law should not be confused. 'It's war,' he says.

The militarization of security forces against crime is more clearly declared as necessary in the series of *Lethal Weapon* films, directed by Richard Donner, starring Mel Gibson and Danny Glover. The first film, in 1987, is centred around the development of a friendly relationship between a black, fifty-something police officer who leads a very conventional middle-class life and does not seem to be aware of the existence of racism in the United States nor of the racist culture of the LAPD, and a Vietnam special forces veteran with strong suicidal tendencies, not because of his military past but because of the death of his wife. Their friendship takes root during the urban warfare that becomes their fight against a group of mercenaries, themselves special forces veterans turned drug traffickers.

The second film, in 1989, depicts their fight against South African diplomats who mount a terrorist campaign in Los Angeles so as to dissuade the police from investigating the drug trafficking they are engaged in to finance the Apartheid government, which is eager for funds because of international sanctions. (The film omits to mention that the boycott dates from the time when the Apartheid government is no longer useful in the fight against Communism in southern Africa.)

In this film, the flow of weapons, drugs and dirty money and the violent practices required to protect them, are mixed in with the common definition of threat that is terrorism and subversive risk, that is everything that evades the legal monopoly of legitimate violence of the official American authorities. The association of terrorism and transnational criminality is shown more clearly again in *Goldeneye* (1995), directed by Martin Campbell, starring Pierce Brosnan, where James Bond prevents the Russian mafia from using a combat satellite inherited from the Soviet Union to beam an electromagnetic wave on the City of London and create widespread financial chaos, just after electronically embezzling an enormous sum of money from the Bank of England.

## Military Intervention

The terrorist threat, nevertheless, remained relatively at the margins of cinema until the release of Edward Zwick's *The Siege*, starring Denzel Washington, in 1998. A small group of Palestinians explode a number of bombs in Manhattan. On the one hand, they want to avenge the manner in which the CIA abandoned them to Saddam Hussein in 1991 after training and preparing them to assassinate the Iraqi leader, while on the other, they want to secure the release of their inspirational sheikh leader secretly captured by the army secret services. The attacks are deadly: the terrorists attack the opera, buses and even blow up the offices of the FBI. The president then decides to declare a State of siege. This decision is followed by the army and special forces occupying the historic immigration area of Brooklyn. The Arab population is locked up in football stadia (something which recalls the images of repression of Pinochet's army in Chile); the American military begin extremely brutal urban warfare operations and torture. The soldiers' excesses are effective against the terrorist cells but transform daily life into a nightmare. At the same time, the FBI ends up arresting the last terrorist and the Army general in charge of the operation for anti-constitutional practices.

The FBI thus re-establishes the normality of daily life, becoming the incarnation of legitimate power against the excesses of the army, which, through its actions, carries out the subversion desired by the terrorists. Terrorist violence, like military violence, are both part of the dislocation of daily life, the 'social counter-project' of the terrorists, which seeks to transform a peaceful society into a terrified one in order to obtain a favourable response to their demands, meanwhile satisfying their hatred and lust for revenge.

With this film, national security cinema again plays the role of alternative history. It questions the historic meaning of national security, which has to uphold the democratic processes vital to the functioning of American society, without slipping into the excessive tyranuty which is the stated aim of those who engage in subversive practices. The film questions the potential for drift inherent in American power, which, by preferring order to law, turns against the Republican and Democratic ideals that legitimize it. In other words, the director questions whether it is possible for those in power to fight the threat they identify without becoming a threat to the society of which they are a part.

This fundamental questioning lends itself to strategic affairs, which had a strong tendency to obscure it between 1993 and 2000 as terrorism emerged as the perfect embodiment of illegitimacy. Nevertheless, the relationship between subversion and violence, legitimacy and illegitimacy, was established by cinema on defence and security institutions who did not want to enter into this debate. In order to do this, the theme of terrorism was completely absent in certain national security films in favour of showing the dilemma between order and chance.

This tension is illustrated by the account of *Crimson Tide* (1995), directed by Tony Scott, with Gene Hackman and Denzel Washington. The scenario centres on a mutiny on board a nuclear submarine. But whilst relations with the Navy were excellent at the time of filming of *Top Gun*, the Navy refused to collaborate at all with the production team for the shooting of the film. Tony Scott then had to have the inside of the submarine built in a studio, through which he gained a freedom of tone and dialogue of a much superior quality. His film was a way of communicating the issue of subversion and its significance to the military – a blind spot in strategic affairs at the time when the film was shot.

*Crimson Tide* shows the State of alert of a nuclear submarine whose crew has to prepare to launch a possible nuclear salvo against a Soviet missile base seized by Russian nationalist extremists. The vessel's commander is 'of the old brigade', trained in the Cold War school and ready to fire without hesitation. His second-in-command belongs to the new generation of commanding officers, highly qualified, not only in action but theory. In his opinion, 'in the nuclear age, the only real enemy is war itself'. Having received an ambiguous order because of a transmission problem, the commander and second-in-command clash about whether to take the decision to launch the missiles or not. The conflict between these two men becomes a mutiny and a conflict between factions, with officers and sub-officers taking one or the other side. It eventually turns out that the decision not to launch the missiles is the right one.

Although the film shows the ability of naval officers to change with the times, the scenario caused a scandal with the military because it presented strategy as a factor in mutiny on board a vessel, a place where it should be absolutely forbidden: it puts the crew's lives in danger, threatens the mission with failure and the institution with discredit.

In addition, the film highlights the question of the obsolescence of chains of command and nuclear doctrines inherited from the Cold War. In the film, the commander reminds his second-in-command that, in the event of a communications black-out, he is expected to launch his weapons. For him, it is about saving the United States from a nuclear missile strike, for his second in command it is about saving the world from a tit-for-tat nuclear exchange between American and Russia that would also sentence the United States to death. The confrontation between the two officers is also a conflict between two views of the world: one that thinks of the defence of the United States in unilateral terms, the other that puts the United States in a world context ruled by interdependence. This conflict of principles is a dead-end because no-one knows what the Russians are doing during this communications black-out. This isolation does not stop the conflict but sends it spiralling, with each side imagining the worst and ally themselves in panic to their own beliefs.

The microcosm of the submarine becomes a synthesis of American strategic affairs and its relationship with the world, a sphere of insular ideas where American strategic autism and the belief in interaction come into conflict.

*Crimson Tide* also belongs to those films which cast doubt on the sphere of doctrinaire ideas that are the basis for the use of power. This doubt becomes a subversive risk whose power is increased by the atmosphere of crisis, because, suddenly, two just as valid strategic concepts are fighting for primacy. This dispute becomes the test of the threat; it demonstrates to what point nuclear technology remains in a very specific area, to the point of taboo.

The introduction of subversive thought into this place is deeply destructive and places nuclear weapons outside the strict controls that makes them fundamentally unusable. Furthermore, the film ends on a text caption stating that, since 1995, submarine commanders can no longer fire without the express order of the president.

Tony Scott's film places itself in this way in the tradition of *The Siege* by reminding the viewer to what extent politicians have to regulate American military power and incorporate very precise ethical rules so as not to become the enemy of those it protects. For these two films, subversion can be caused by an aggressive military power that no longer knows how to orientate itself, being deprived of worthy opponents this blind force becomes difficult to bring under control. Strategic power in fact threatens to completely change the civilian, military, political and social order under its charge.

This theme of the risk of subversion spreading in the midst of military society is particularly energized by the disappearance of threat and the return to the isolationism that characterized the Clinton years. Strategic affairs, the military and security institutions turning in on themselves created many internal tensions which were just waiting for a pretext to crystallize. These tensions inside the military community reflected the fear of an armed rebellion that could call into question the unity of society. Cinema expresses these tensions, reprising the theme of mutiny but also that of terrorism.

It is Michael Bay, in filming *The Rock* in 1995, with Nicholas Cage and Sean Connery, who, through a fictional account, reveals the most complete synthesis of this problem. A team of reconnaissance marine commandos seize a stock of chemical weapons, before taking tourists hostage on the island of Alcatraz and training the missiles charged with chemical warheads on San

Francisco. Their commander demands the Pentagon officials recognise that his men were abandoned by the authorities into the hands of the Iraqis in 1991 as release secret funds to their families, all to make the institution pay for its long silence on the pointless sacrifice of men who were entirely devoted to their nation. A marine commando, accompanied by a chemical weapons specialist and a former British agent who has been kept in solitary confinement for years – he was the only person to manage to escape from Alcatraz – get onto the island. The rebels kill the commando after a failed attempt to reconcile the two units' commanders, who are arguing about the duty of military obedience compared to the duty to the nation's gratitude. The idealistic rebels end up launching a warhead on San Francisco in order to obtain their ransom, becoming mercenaries in the process. The missiles will be destroyed by the young chemist and the old British agent just at the moment when the president gives the order to bomb Alcatraz.

Michael Bay presents the rupture of the link between the community and the core of the army in the form of sedition, the military version of civil war. But whilst the brothers-in-arms bloodily turn on each other in the name of different concepts about their relationship with politicians and the nation, the integrity of society is at stake in their fight. The social order is then in mortal danger from those who have the monopoly of legitimate armed violence.

This series of films on the theme of subversion poses the problem of the relationships between the means of the army and the police forces in relation to the always imagined ends, that is the maintenance of civilian peace during a period when a clearly identified outside threat is absent. American political culture, no longer seeing an equivalent counter-balance to the national security system, then condemns its own inherent tyrannical potential. However, even if the threat remained confused, the Clinton period was also characterized by increased technological development of the defence apparatus, commonly called a 'Revolution in Military Affairs' (RMA). National security cinema would elaborate this through science fiction.

# 6

# PEARL HARBOR SYNDROME AND THE
# FABLES OF TECHNOLOGY, 1986–2000

The Gulf War set in motion a large-scale technological transformation because of the role played by space hardware and the new effectiveness it gives to air power, eavesdropping, the observation of enemy forces and fine-tuning of operational plans.

In parallel also to the issue of the strategic dimension of subversion, the question of technology dominated American strategic affairs from 1992 to 2000 to a large extent. At a time when the whole of the American defence and security system was subjected to a constant political pressure to modernize by integrating new technology, extraterrestrials and Nature become the essential themes of the definition of threat and a way of promoting new American strength combined with space power.

## Pearl Harbor Syndrome

This fear of incapacitation stems from what we will call 'Pearl Harbor syndrome'. The battle of Pearl Harbor was a key event in the construction of American strategic memory. When Japanese fighters carried out a dawn raid on a US Navy base on 7 December 1941 and destroyed a large part of the American war fleet, not only did they inflict an operational defeat on the American army, but they brought about the fear of having suffered a crippling defeat. In effect, during the few days required to evaluate the damage and to get the national mobilization of America under way, high-ranking politicians and military commanders lived in fear of having been rendered helpless by a single preventive strike that could have destroyed their capacity to intervene in the Pacific.

This terror of being incapacitated became a recurring motif in American formulation of strategy, particularly between the middle of the Reagan years and 2001. It affected every area in which the national security system operated. This strategic syndrome was started by Reagan's plans for an anti-missile space shield in order to avoid a *'nuclear Pearl Harbor'*. In 1997, the

Senate Commission on future ballistic threats, headed by Donald Rumsfeld, envisaged the scenario of a *'Pearl Harbor by ballistic missile'*; Space Command, whose doctrine revolves around protecting space hardware claimed to fear an attack on them that would trigger off a *space Pearl Harbor*. At the same time, the entry of American society into the 'information age' makes a number of civilian and military prospectors fear a *cyber Pearl Harbor*, even an *asymmetrical Pearl Harbor*. There is therefore a danger of 'Pearl Harbor' at the time when a threat, which suddenly emerges without being detected or foreseen, risks stretching operations or equipment capabilities, leading the United States unable to react or conduct its affairs and defend itself.

The surprise attack is experienced as a major risk not only for the army but also for American society: it could make its security and cohesion lethally disorganized, before which the strategic system would be powerless. A popular strategic scenario consists of imagining a complete dislocation of social and political life if communication satellites, through which the flow of information passes, were neutralized.

However, another essential function of creating this syndrome is to justify the ideologies of security and defence, by helping the national security elite to 'scaremonger' and popularize this fear by way of creating the main strategic direction that not only adopts and acquires weapons systems, but also the continued social and economic mobilization that underlie them.

Since the Reagan years (1980–88), a whole branch of national security cinema has specialized in the treatment of this syndrome. The main film of this time is James Cameron's *Aliens* in 1986, starring Sigourney Weaver and Michael Biehn. A planet is bought by a mining company which quickly loses contact with its colonists. A rescue expedition is dispatched, comprising Lieutenant Ripley (who confirms that the colonists have been attacked by the same creature that killed her crew and destroyed her ship in Ridley Scott's *Alien* in 1979), a company representative and a battalion of space marines who have great confidence in their fire power and aggression. They arrive on the planet, find the devastated colony in which only a little girl has survived. They are then ambushed by 'perfect predators', who leave them stranded on the planet without any means of getting off, virtually without weapons or provisions.

In American strategic thought, this sequence symbolizes a surprise incapacitating and organic strike on a space colony, which transforms the marines from their status as masters of fire-power and warfare technology to that of stranded colonists in the middle of a hostile environment, surrounded by an enemy adapted to this terrain. They thus find themselves back on the Frontier. From supreme and confident colonizers they become the prey. Pearl Harbor syndrome thus proves itself to be the driving force of a call to arms for survival and a strategic reaction. The marines regain their willingness to fight and seize the initiative again by killing the 'Queen Mother' of the Aliens, but also vitrifying the planet by a nuclear bombardment. 'That way, we'll be sure!' the last officer, a corporal, and the civilian head of the operation, declares.

This anti-military and anti-colonial attack on the Aliens comes to its 'logical' conclusion: their nuclear extermination. The aggressors are victims of a nuclear strike launched by the Americans. In fact, as the film clearly shows, the syndrome is an essential means of justifying and legitimising the pursuit of power, which cannot be separated from the technological race that the United States is running against itself.

The military and technological precision of the film depends on the work carried out before James Cameron started filming, which involved extensive research on modern weaponry and urban warfare tactics before even starting to write the script. In addition, the preparation of the actors set in motion the current trend of military professionals systematically training actors before shooting starts. (Today, certain actors, like Angelina Jolie, agree to shoot a national security film on the understanding that the training they will undergo will help them in their choice of subsequent roles.)

## Filming the Modernization of the American Army

Ten years after this film, the American strategic system was involved in RMA (Revolution in Military Affairs), that is that the American army was moving towards new technology, integrating in particular the space dimension in order to increase its capacity for precision, speed and deployment all over the world.

A key plank of RMA was to require the Army, Air Force and the Navy to work together, to coordinate themselves, but also to complement one another. American strategists refer to it as a project of *jointness*. The need for it was made clear by the fiasco in 1983 of the invasion of the island of Grenada during which American warships bombarded their own ground troops after they had landed. The Army and the Navy not having compatible communication systems, the commander of ground troops had to call headquarters at the Pentagon from a telephone box exposed to enemy fire so the order to stop firing could be sent to the commander of the fleet. Furthermore, this episode constitutes the end of Clint Eastwood's 1986 film *Heartbreak Ridge*; this fiasco, however overshadowed by the victory, nevertheless fuelled the idea that the military machine needed reforming.

Then, during the Gulf War, the immense efforts deployed by Norman Schwarzkopf's command to get good coordination between the forces, but also to get them all to carry out what was expected of them and not what each wanted to do in terms of their own view of the conflict, only reinforced the idea that was taking shape in RMA. RMA justified itself by the concept that it made the military more reactive a lot more quickly. It is through RMA that the Air Force launched its offensive on the Pentagon by asserting itself like the army as the best-equipped to introduce the requirements of *jointness* and reactivity within its very ranks and in relation to its dealings with other armed services.

This self-promotion of the Air Force was so effective that it is at the heart of the strategic discourse of *Independence Day* (1996), by Roland Emmerich, starring Will Smith and Jeff Goldblum. The film begins on 2 July: massive spaceships position themselves over major cities in the world and we follow what happens in Washington, New York and Los Angeles. The president of the United States, a former fighter squadron leader during the Gulf War, and his advisers are in a State of uncertainty. A genius computer operator, David, realizes that the signals exchanged between the spaceships are a countdown. He manages to warn the White House and to be evacuated from Washington with the president in the presidential plane, Air Force One. One minute later, all the major cities are destroyed at the same time by an enormous ray of energy sent from the spaceships. On 3 July, what remains of the cities populations are homeless in the desert. A counter-attack is launched by the Air Force, ground troops having been annihilated. The squadrons smash into the spaceships protective fields and those of the extraterrestrial fighters. It is a bloodbath.

However, the director of the CIA informs the president of the existence of a secret base where a downed space craft has been kept since the 1950s. David and an Air Force pilot then prepare a counter attack in the base, after a nuclear strike against the aggressors has failed. David perfects a computer virus capable of destroying the computer that activates the protective fields from the mother ship. Once completed, the Air Force launches a conventional attack. On the evening of 3 July, civilian pilots are quickly drafted in to the Air Force, which becomes a militia like those who liberated the 13 colonies from British (sic) oppression.

On 4 July, Independence Day, the cyber-attack works, F-16s begin the attack on the destructive enemy and, with great loss of life, destroy the spaceships. The tactics are communicated to surviving air forces, Russian, Chinese and Israel-Iraqi (who have joined up in the Sinai).

This film, which shows Pearl Harbor syndrome in a radicalized form, was a media, political, strategic and popular event all at once. It was the hit of the summer of 1996 in the United States with nearly 20,000,000 ticket sales, but also in Israel. In the autumn, it attracted nearly 5,000,000 cinema-goers in

France. It sparked enthusiastic responses in the United States among very diverse groups.

For example, cinema-goers in the Midwest stood up and shouted with joy at the destruction of New York city. This most traditional population saw New York as a hotbed of atheists and sinners and the seat of Wall Street, a major threat to American agriculture and rural, post Frontier traditions. Among the military, the film was seen by nearly the whole of the marine corps, the president of the joint-command, the right-hand man of the president, being shown for the first time as a marine.

But, above all, *Independence Day* is an 'Air Force film', even if its production was not officially backed by the US Air Force. By beating the extraterrestrials with a combination of air power, space power and cyber power, and by ensuring the switch from strategic nuclear weapons to the use of tactical mini-bombs, the Air Force saves the United States and thus the world. The other armed forces are not even shown and the rest of the national security system is restricted to the director of the CIA, a man of limited competence. The Air Force, however, is shown as the only armed service capable of combining tactical and technological expertise, but also the necessary heroism, for such a difficult fight and to respond to the strategic demands of defending the whole of the United States.

The heroism of Air Force is stressed even more by the film's strong theological script, conveyed by a whole range of imagery borrowed from the Old Testament. The cities are destroyed by 'fire from the sky', which recalls the fate of Sodom and Gomorrah; the American people take refuge in the desert, in large mobile homes like a new Hebrew people. The people are attacked by extraterrestrials, who are compared with locusts, another form of divine retribution. The computer virus employed against the mother ship symbolizes the catapult allowing the defeat of the modern Goliath from a distance. It was perfected by a computer scientist called David, who is congratulated by a patriarchal president.

In fact, *Independence Day* clearly depicts the elevation of the American people to the status of the new elect, whose first demonstration of legitimacy is the distribution to the armies of the world of the means of destroying the alien vessel. In so doing, the United States 'illuminates' the world with its saving light like the legend of the City upon a hill, a new Jerusalem which embodies the hope of mankind. The film blurs in this way all the boundaries between theology, politics and strategy, for the purpose of a tale of the testing, regeneration and election of America among the nations of the world.

In the context of this dream of renewal of the alliance between God and man in America, the Air Force becomes a celestial army and a bringer of technological and military and also spiritual hope. It leads the combat against the delinquent creatures which carry celestial fire. It destroys them, a metaphor of the dethronement of Lucifer, the 'bringer of light'. This heavenly dimension of the Air Force is not new; its creation as a separate service from the Army was supported by the evangelical senators of the Midwest, attracted by the fact that an army could deploy in the skies to go and fight evil across the seas. This incomparable characteristic of the Air Force makes it the ideal military tool for fighting the hordes of extraterrestrials who recall Satan declaring: 'I am legion', and preventing the end of the world.

As Sebastien Fath[1] demonstrates, *Independence Day* is at the junction of a traditional millenarian vision in the United States, demanding the individual to prepare for Judgement Day and the fight against Satan, and post-millenarianism, insofar as America becomes a matchless commodity. This theological ideology combines with the strategic vision that the United States has of itself and of its relationship with the world.

Pearl Harbor syndrome thus becomes a divine examination which affirms the political pre-eminence of the United States and legitimacy, at the time when the American strategic system is preparing itself for a new pursuit of the militarization of space.

The increase in power of the military/space sector thus coincided with the entire process of revising the definition of threat during the years that separate the Gulf War and 11 September 2001. It is expressed by a spatial definition of threat and the increase in spatial problematics and traditional dilemmas like Pearl Harbor syndrome and the question of subversion.

## Shaping the World

These years were also the time when the strategic ideology of 'shaping the world' was created. It was only made official by President Clinton on 27 January 2000 during a State of the Union address where he declared: 'To realize the full opportunities of the new economy, we must reach beyond our own borders, to shape the revolution that is tearing down barriers and building new networks among nations and individuals, economies and cultures: globalization. It is the central reality of our time.... We must be at the center of every vital global network...'

The essential idea of this ideology of imposing globalization according to American interests is the realization that, the world not corresponding to American standards and principles, it is necessary to use global methods and initiate relevant hegemonic practices, at the level of international society, so that it can adapt to the American system (and not the other way around).

This new theory of political dominance takes into account the impact of new technologies and their effect on the definition of threat, vulnerability and security, by means of the problems linked to information strategies, which cannot be separated from questions about space.

These questions about space are at the heart of Roger Spottiswoode's 1997 James Bond film *Tomorrow Never Dies*, starring Piers Brosnan. James Bond has to fight a media mogul (clearly inspired by Ted Turner, founder, chairman and managing director of CNN) who, using his satellites, mixes up the guidance systems of British and American warships in the South China Sea and transmits orders to Chinese fighter planes to create a series of incidents designed to trigger a Sino-American war. He would then be able to film it live for his rolling news network. Furthermore, he declares:

> Words are the new weapons, satellites the new artillery. Caesar had his legions. Napoleon had his armies. I have my divisions. TV. News. Magazines. And by midnight tonight I will have reached and influenced more people than anyone else in the history of this planet save God himself. And the best he ever managed was the Sermon on the Mount.

James Bond will put things in order and the media mogul will die horribly; the threat from space and subversion, embodied by the spatial device of 'info-war', will similarly be wiped out.

Again, the film effectively reprises the way in which strategic affairs have never stopped criss-crossing the different themes of threat around issues associated with 'info-dominance': GPS modifications, cyber-influence, the sensory isolation of decision-makers, manipulations of public opinion. So many themes are contained within the preoccupations and official documents produced by Space Command. In this film, the emergence of a trans-national private space power goes hand-in-hand with the idea that it is possible to engage in subversive activities at an international level, to the extent that the American State and her allies are deprived of their decision-making capacity and induced, without them knowing, into taking part in the subversive scheme that is playing one off against the other.

This renewal of national security cinema at the time the *shaping the world* ideology and info-dominance strategies was being developed, also has a wider appeal as space technology strengthened its position in American strategy: controlling Nature. The trend was particularly noticeable from 1998.

In that year, Space Command found itself given the task of watching out for asteroids that could hit Earth. This widening of military assignments to the surveillance of Nature herself goes back to the age-old fear felt by Americans about the fragility of their society in the face of the environment. While the feeling of American vulnerability is generally expressed by the obsession of having 'everything under control', particularly in the strategic domain, by the increase in plans and the disproportionate accumulation of superior material, Nature escapes this desire to control. Its ever probable excesses make the strategic system fear an equivalent war scenario emerging in the land where peace should reign and Nature should be tamed.

This dilemma is at the heart of the drama of Michael Bay's *Armageddon* (1998), starring Bruce Willis. A giant asteroid, preceded by a meteor shower, is going to crash into Earth in 18 days. Because of its size, all life could be wiped out. A team of oil industry drillers is quickly trained by NASA to be sent onto the asteroid to dig a hole where a nuclear weapon will be placed, the explosion of which will eradicate the threat. The team, sent on a space shuttle, must cope with both the surface of the asteroid – the embodiment of all nature's hostility to man – and the contradictory orders coming from Earth, which could be blown up because of a dispute between the military and the workers.

The asteroid is the Frontier in the most radical sense, the place where man can only impose his technology or die, without any compromise being possible. In addition, as always in American strategic thought, this struggle with Nature, which must be *shaped*, and created for human needs through the combination of industrial, spatial and nuclear technologies, is shown as being also a struggle with God, who demands a sacrifice so as to bestow the role of saviours of all humanity on the American 'pioneers'. Furthermore, the head of the expedition, Bruce Willis, sacrifices himself to ensure the survival of his daughter, his son-in-law, the United States and the world by activating *in extremis* the bomb that blows up the asteroid.

Parallel to the action on the asteroid, the film is composed of numerous sequences showing all the peoples of the Earth united in the threat of death and praying for the success of the American astronauts. What is more, this prayer is begun in person by the president of the United States on television and radio stations the world over.

After military civilizations across the world are reshaped under the orders of the Air Force in *Independence Day*, *Armageddon* puts forward the vision of a *shaped* world, refashioned, united in a worldwide prayer for the success of the United States and saved by the synergy of *space power* and the heroic individualism of Americans.

## From Space Power to Space Shield

These different works stress the offensive dimension of militarizing space, but the proposal of this type of American space power breathes new life into the debate about its defensive counterpart, the anti-missile space shield, now labelled 'National Missile Defense' (NMD) in the 1990s. Until now, this formidable programme of the defensive militarization of space has not resulted in anything worthwhile operationally and it will, in all likelihood, be like this for the next 25 years. The NMD programme had, nevertheless, numerous and wide-ranging effects in the aerospace industry: new technologies, optics, satellite and ballistic satellite research, not to mention the Keynesian and covert support to the revival of the universities, that is the massive State aid in the land of supposedly accomplished liberalization. For, if the militarization of space does not require the development of NMD, the project cannot be conceived of without *space power*. It is subject to constant and inevitable justification. For example, Bill Clinton, at the start of his second term in office, was keen to appease Republican hawks and the military who were taken with the programme, so as to not have to manage a crisis between the civilians and the military at the end of a presidency full of internal political controversy.

This justification requires the endlessly reiterated assertion of a ballistic or airborne threat that only the strategic weapon of NMD could incapacitate. This assertion requires unleashing the threat of State intention; but in effect what State today would have the political and military will, and to what end, to launch one or more ballistic missiles against the United States, knowing that the reprisals would be of the same type, but a lot more severe? (On the level of know-how and infrastructure, mastering ballistic technology has nothing to do with hijacking a commercial aeroplane with craft knives!)

This shift from the threat defined by political hostility, the perils of Nature or divine anger, to a threat identified with a technological potential, strictly speaking runs through a certain number of official documents, but is extremely difficult to depict on screen. In effect, strategic threat inevitably implies the relationship with the war required to eradicate it, when, in fact, technology is not in itself an enemy; this myth of threatening ballistic technology if it is not controlled by the American system does not escape the prism of the silver screen. What is more, NMD presents another sizeable strategic problem, inasmuch as it does not exist and will not exist for at least 25 years. It is a fabrication for scientific, industrial, economic, diplomatic and hegemonic use, but on the level of real power, it remains only the fantasy of perfect protection resulting from the convergence between the Messianic hope of Ronald Reagan and science-fiction make-believe.

This State of affairs is particularly evident in the only two 'major NMD films' – *Thirteen Days* and *Pearl Harbor* – where neither missiles nor satellites are seen. Roger Donaldson's *Thirteen Days* (2000), starring Kevin Costner, is inspired by the account of the Cuban missile crisis written by John F Kennedy's policy adviser Kenny O'Donnell. The film highlights the rise in tension in the midst of the White House and the Pentagon as the fear of the missiles increases. The missiles are never seen but are constantly evoked as devices threatening the devastation of American society in the same way that modern weapons wrought havoc on the French, British, German and Russian armies in 1914. This metaphor is not gratuitous; it is a device to evoke the risk of the end of the world.

The film accentuates the idea, however, that the political victory belongs to the person who will best read and influence the will of his opponent by playing the information game in the media and on television. Information comes above all from aero-spatial observation. The stake, for the Americans, is to persuade the Soviets to think about installing nuclear weapons in Cuba. Thus, news management allows the threat posed by the missiles to be virtualized. The concept of the anti-missile shield functions in much the same way: it is said to be obsolete by the very people who exploit it for their own strategic advantage.

The question about the need for an NMD is expressed in less abstract fashion in Michael Bay's *Pearl Harbor* (2000). The battle is presented as a Japanese victory of operations and information. The film shows preparations for the attack from a 'war of information' perspective, the Japanese drowning the Americans in a flood of information from which they fail to extract the most essential part. The need for *space power* is evoked by the 'disappearance' of the Japanese fleet in an area of the Pacific Ocean the size of Asia and nicknamed the 'black hole', where it frustrates American vigilance and observational capacities. Finally, the American fleet is portrayed as slow and unwieldy, incapable of reacting with the required State of readiness or of employing its informational abilities advisedly, compared with the air forces, whose heroism is supposed to have dissuaded Tojo Hideki from launching his third wave of attack. In so doing, he does not finish off the American fleet. In fact, the Japanese and American air fleets are portrayed as two sides of the same coin: able to launch a force which is rapid, precise, and discriminating (a Japanese pilot signals to some children to go and shelter and, later, Doolittle's American reprisal raid on Tokyo is only supposed to aim for industrial targets), and totally superior to any defence system, leading to a minimum of collateral damage, unless the opposite is desired.

*Pearl Harbor* unites the main points about the legends of threat and air supremacy; it is the metaphor for the need for the defence system to change and modernize and acquire the means for an effective defence against a possible technological threat from the skies. In this respect, the key scene of the film is an astonishing shot, following a bomb falling towards an American warship until it hits the bridge. During this shot-sequence, the threat is strictly one about capability, it has no given political identity; the screen is filled by a self-sufficient and sophisticated technological object whose *raison d'être* is to destroy its target.

*Pearl Harbor* is thus the portrayal of the American fantasy of war imagined in terms of strict technological confrontation between unequally sophisticated and modern weapons systems, in order to achieve a purity of combat stripped of the dilemma of the life and death of the soldiers sanctified by their martyrdom. American unilateralism finds its legitimacy in it as well as the pursuit of air weapons and the obligation of losing no more men in combat.

But if this film is fully involved in the Republican hawks' offensive in favour of NMD, for reasons as strange and complex as those shown in the film, *space power* is equally the subject of a conflicting debate, even in Hollywood, the ins and outs of which are demonstrated through the 'fables of *space power*': *Starship Troopers* (1997) *The Matrix* (1998) and *Space Cowboys* (2000).

While the 1990s were years when air power increased in strength, its predicament was also the subject of serious critiques, of which the first large-scale one is Paul Verhoeven's *Starship Troopers*, starring Casper Van Diem and Denise Richards. The film begins by showing Earth under total American hegemony, united and homogenized after an immense shaping of the world. The world starts a war against a race of giant extraterrestrial insects. It is a total war, on the ground where it is bloody and leads to massive human losses, but also in the air, space and information; this last area has acquired an extreme degree of sophistication, headed by a 'psy corps' made up of telepathic agents who, through their powers, are able to read the minds of the enemy and, eventually, influence the people with whom they have 'connected'. They are a metaphor for the info-dominance capabilities that Space Command is trying to develop.

But above all the film puts to the fore the risk of society turning fascist if it lets itself become too absorbed by its army, symbolized here by *space power*. In this sense, *Starship Troopers* is not a classic national security film, but a strategic fable recalling the paradoxes of a power that destroys itself through bad government. It is in the tradition of strategic legends, inspired by the fear felt in the face of American military nuclear power, the most important of which are *Planet of the Apes, Wargames* and *Terminator*. The dimension of fable and allegory is adopted particularly when members of the psy corps are shown; having corrupted the power that *space power* is used to attain, they are shown dressed in uniforms directly inspired by those of the Gestapo. It must be remembered in this respect that Paul Verhoeven, like a number of influential and inventive European intellectuals, left Europe in order to benefit from the opportunities offered by the American system, which recognizes the abilities and 'added-value' of artists and thinkers. Insofar as through his film he is involved in American strategic affairs, his path in life corresponds with people like Henry Kissinger, a German-Jewish immigrant, or Zbigniew Brzezinski, a Polish Catholic immigrant who advocates putting pivotal Eurasian States under the supervision of the United States.

The essential strategic themes set out by *space power* are those of the 'information war' and 'info-dominance', which are recounted in fabulist form in *The Matrix* (1998), by the Wachowski brothers, starring Keanu Reeves. In this film, reality is denounced because it is just an illusion generated by the matrix, a network of supercomputers which has transformed humanity into energy resources, enclosing the vast majority of mankind in cocoons where cerebral cortexes are little more than inert 'batteries'. Only a few small groups of human resistance fighters try to destroy the matrix while avoiding its agents. In this, they search for 'The One', the Chosen One, who will guide them towards the centre of the matrix and destroy it. The One turns out to be a young computer hacker capable of turning the reality of the matrix against itself. The film is a fable about the power bases manipulation of the rules of reality during the cyberspace age, which has become one of the essential prisms for constructing and perceiving reality.

*The Matrix* questions the influence of cyberstrategies, which could completely distort relations with individuals, the world and power and have fantastic 'invisible' subversive consequences, not to further a terrorist cause but to further an expansionist project of the power of the State, to the advantage of oligarchies who control the strategic means arising out of *space power*.

This questioning of the strategic consequences of *space power* not on the world but on the United States itself, is presented in the cinema and strategy in head-on and radical fashion in *Space Cowboys* (2000), directed by and starring Clint Eastwood, with Tommy Lee Jones, Donald Sutherland and James Garner. While films like *Armageddon* and *Independence Day* affirm the renewal of the United States election, as well as the legitimacy of American technological and strategic power, Clint Eastwood examines this conviction by questioning the Nature of *space power*.

Four septuagenarians, former members of the Air Force and the only ones to still remember such obsolete technology, are sent into orbit by NASA to repair a Russian communication satellite. Once there, they discover that the satellite in question is in fact a nuclear missile platform that has targeted the United States since the end of the 1960s, and whose orbit is weakening, hence the urgency and secrecy of the Russian request. But the technology required to construct this platform can only have been developed by the KGB by stealing American technical plans. The true origin of this both spatial and nuclear deadly threat is thus none other than the American national security system, whose unregulated transfer of technology has allowed the instruments of Soviet threat to spread. The satellite is finally reorientated towards the moon, at the cost of the life of one of the crew, in order to avoid an accidental nuclear disaster.

Clint Eastwood sees a strategic threat in *space power* because of its combination with nuclear strategies and the bureaucratic secrecy that surrounds it. *Space power* only reinforces the power of the State while at the same time being at the heart of that secrecy. As it involves a technology which is hard to control and whose effects are to make the planet a target, the risks of accident cannot be tolerated. In fact, space strategies represent the potential for unintentional threats by the national security system.

In this way, the national security system creates the risk that the technologies it has itself developed, that it has abandoned and that no-one can control any more, could trigger off a *space and nuclear Pearl Harbor*. Comparisons are inevitable between the observations of Clint Eastwood's film and the curious incident of the fire in the Russian Space Command in 2001, which forced the Russian authorities to ask for American help in order to keep control of their satellite network.

Nevertheless, while certain powerful sections of the American strategic system are seduced by space and caught up in the illusion of global, omniscient and omnipotent power that the militarisation of space seems to offer, an area readily adopted by the cinema, the question of real combat, on the ground, and the limits it imposes on the spread of American strategic power, returns with a vengeance. This fundamental question is not asked officially by the army, but by the cinema.

# 7

# SAVING GROUND COMBAT, 1987–2000

In 1987, General Colin Powell, after being national security adviser to Ronald Reagan, saw himself given the responsibility of leading a review into the future size of the American army. This was labelled the *bottom up review*. The former army general represents a whole generation of officers and soldiers marked by the disastrous use of ground forces during the Vietnam War and particularly by the losses that ensued.

This mistrust of ground combat is expressed in the same year with John McTiernan's *Predator* (1987), which follows a group of army special forces sent to the jungle of a Central American country in order to rescue American soldiers and political leaders who have been captured by Guerillas. Mission accomplished, they are tracked by an extraterrestrial fighter made invisible thanks to a 'chameleon-like' camouflage system, which kills them one-by-one. The last survivor, Arnold Schwarzenegger, then transforms himself into a 'prehistoric warrior', a primitive creature who reconnects with the instinct of ancient hunters to hunt down his counterpart. By acting in this way, he loses his soldier's identity, defined by the uniform and the inscription in a chain of command, to become a warrior, whose psychology is determined by his relation to fighting, and not to discipline and obedience. Ground combat is characterized therefore by the risk of human casualties, but also by its inability to keep even its best principles.

This regression of the military to the warrior figure is a direct allusion to *Apocalypse Now* and to the risk of madness that takes hold of soldiers caught up in a war situation whose purpose escapes them. *Predator* who the last film for a while to depict military ground combat because of the global geopolitical and strategic situation, the structural development of which was to dry up the theme of American-led ground war for several years.

## Glory Versus the Disappearance of the USSR

The decline of the Soviet threat is illustrated by the exhaustion of the theme of war in movies of the period. This immediately causes a problem concerning the maintenance of social unity as the public is deprived of the concensus built around threat. This identity crisis is potentially crucial, the American strategic memory keeping alive the memory of the American Civil War, the result of a vast internal process of separation which risked killing off the very concept of Union.

This dilemma is the subject of Edward Zwick's *Glory* (1990), starring Denzel Washington, Matthew Broderick and Morgan Freeman. It recounts the creation of the first battalion of black soldiers during the American Civil War. A Federal officer becomes conscious of the need to involve the black population, if only because of the enormous losses brought about by the battles; the film shows their training, the officers efforts to get them to fight, and finally the complete destruction of the batallion as they try to take a Yankee position.

The political message of the film is clear. If the American Civil War was a moment of violent separation inside the American nation, this movement was 'compensated' by the Army's work integrating black people, who fought with weapons and the involvement of these new recruits against this break-up. The fight that the American nation must lead is thus one for unity and integration, even in the absence of an outside enemy, by preventing the certain sections of its population being demonised. The film was a great success in the military, to the extent that Colin Powell had a giant version of the poster put in his office in the Pentagon, thus confirming the glorious arrival of the American army, which in and through the ground combat required to preserve the Union, became the heart of the American nation in its modern and integrated form.

American cinema audiences understand from the concept of Edward Zwick's film that the separatist movements which hounded the American army during and after the Vietnam War are finally spent. In Vietnam black soldiers and white officers confronted and even killed each other before going into combat zones and in numerous barrack buildings both inside and outside the United States. Zwick's film casts the army at the forefront of the movement to integrate and pacify society, in this time when not war, but the concept of it, is redundant.

This last part of the message is emphasized by the way in which the director films the combat, with a violence unequalled since Sam Peckinpah: there are scenes of mutilation and ultra-rapid, bloody deaths, where men are forced into committing the most extreme violence. In effect, until then, American war films are, in general, very codified, particularly in the way in which fighting, injuries, hand-to-hand combat and death is portrayed. That is the terrifying reality of the ground combat of the time. The American soldier is someone pleasant, heroic, idealistic, perhaps a little 'unpolished', who kills properly and is wounded, whether fatally or not, just as decently, knowing how to conduct himself when in pain. When there is a problem of cowardice or conscience, he is either killed by the enemy or by his comrades for reasons of legitimate defence, or he realizes his mistakes and returns to the 'primary group', this band of men forged by the shared experience of operations since leaving the barracks. These constant themes cut across practically the whole of American ground war cinema from 1942 to 1989. Yet, the Vietnam War had such a destructive effect on the different methods of creating consensus that it made possible several works that put forward another perspective on the actual reality of combat.

The two most important films of this period are *The Wild Bunch* (1968) and *Cross of Iron* (1977), both by Sam Peckinpah. At the end of the 1960s, this filmmaker revolutionized the way of filming violence, and particularly military violence. A difficult character, Peckinpah could not stand the way studio 'egg heads' took it upon themselves to interfere in the scenarios he had chosen to adapt, to the extent that one day he went in to his producer's office with a chain saw and turned the furniture into bits of wood. His hard-fought independence thus achieved, he could then film *Cross of Iron*, a tale of the gradual disintegration of a German units on the Russian front in 1943, through both battles with the enemy and hostility between the men of the unit themselves.

Undoubtedly, scenes of such violence had never been seen on screen before. (We could ask if they have been surpassed since.) The fighting is divided into two precise stages: one army unit approaching the other, under fire, them the confrontation between the men in a mass of hand-to-hand fighting. Sam Peckinpah films close up – bodies are ripped apart by bullets, and men must become like the possessed to beat their enemy by killing or wounding them in any way possible. This shows the battlefield for what it is, a very short-lived place in which the intention is not to create but to destroy, by emphasizing the explosion of bodies by bullets, gunfire and shelling.

This film, made while the Vietnam War was still in progress, gave a clear idea to the audience of what American soldiers were having to face, due to the enemy and their own leaders. The government resumption of control of the useless military between 1975 and 1980 made this film stand out from the official cinema annals of strategic affairs at the time.

Sam Peckinpah is cross of iron breached the prescriptive Hollywood system. Thirteen years later, Edward Zwick was inspired by it to film the American Civil War, but it was no longer a question of condemning the inhumanity of war, it involved aggrandising the courage of white and black soldiers who managed to set aside their fears and prejudices, to face the horror of combat united, thus displaying the fundamental role of the federal army as the heart of the nation.

## The Ideology of 'Zero Losses'

Then came the remarkable military victory of the Gulf War, with paradoxical effects for the Army and the Navy. In effect, the pincer movement around the

Iraqi Army by the US Army and the Marines was all the more glorious because the Iraqi Army was worn down by five weeks of intensive bombardment that made them lose all cohesion and willingness to fight. By its fire power, the Army destroyed or forced the final combat units to flee without having had to engage in anything other than several rear-guard actions, even if some of them were fierce.

Ground combat effectively presents numerous problems and questions for strategists and American political leaders because it comes down to the risk of losses, and the sudden emergence of the 'zero losses' ideology at the time of the Gulf War declared any loss unacceptable. The origins of this ideology are difficult to establish clearly, but in their respective memoirs, Norman Schwarzkopf, Colin Powell, James Baker and George Bush are united in celebrating the incredibly low numbers of American soldiers killed, and make of it one of the essential criteria of the victory.

The ideology of 'zero losses' emerged from the reaction to the 50,000 American dead in the Vietnam War. The pointlessness of all these deaths endangered the cohesion of the nation and society and energized all forms of protest at that time in the United States. The social and political effects became the symbol and the definition of threat for the American political and military elite, who were from then on filled with the horror of defeat, which was largely identified with the risk of losses, and thus illegitimacy. As a result, the benchmark of victory became 'zero losses'. This new standard was avidly adopted by the national security *establishment*: it explained the speed of the American withdrawal from the UN forces in Mogadishu in October 1993 following the death of 18 commandos and Delta Force soldiers. At the same time, this standard of 'zero losses' gave defence industries an additional way of promoting more and more sophisticated war and weapon systems that required spiralling financial resources.

From a European perspective, this deep feeling of inadequacy between the military and the risk of losses is very odd. However, it is at the heart of Edward Zwick's next film, *Courage Under Fire* (1996), starring Denzel Washington and Meg Ryan. The film, the only production to recall the fighting in Kuwait, but which was made five years after the war and where we do not see a single Iraqi, follows the inquiry led by a tank regiment colonel into the death of a helicopter pilot during Operation 'Desert Storm', where he personally led his battalion into battle and accidentally fired on one of his own tanks, killing a friend, a memory that haunts him and is driving him to the brink of alcoholism. He discovers that the tank driver captain was killed by his own men who wanted to flee while he ordered them to hold their position around the helicopter waiting for daybreak. The heroism of this 'unknown driver' inspires him: he decides to break the military code of silence about his own accident and to inform the parents of his brother-in-arms that he was killed by 'friendly fire'. During his investigation, the colonel realizes that his reaction after the accident was the spur-of-the-moment adjustment of a tactic that saved the unit from an Iraqi bombardment and he understands that he himself acted like a hero. He can now get back on the straight and narrow and turn away from the bottle.

This film, by showing the Iraqi soldiers as shadows, could be addressed the same way that a senator remarked to General Schwarzkopf about the official report into the behaviour of the American army during the Gulf War: 'It is a shame he didn't mention the Iraqis!' In the words of the famous strategist Edward Luttwak, it poses the problem of the cohesion of the 'post-heroic' American army. This cohesion is felt in all its fragility because it is threatened by the fear of losses, however small, during an operation, which are felt like a betrayal. If the American Army aspires to operational perfection and invulnerability, none of its hopes can be achieved; one contradicts the other. The film clearly shows that trauma comes from interacting with the enemy, which creates this moment of confusion that Clausewitz calls the 'fog of war',[1] and which leaves American soldiers with a feeling of powerlessness not unlike a State of shock.

Edward Zwick also sets himself up as the spokesman for the disarray of the Army, which provided all the military equipment and specialists to operate it, something which allowed the filming of the battle scenes with the tanks to be undoubtedly the most impressive ever seen on screen. This use of technology acts on behalf of an account of one superior officer's disarray, who does not manage to accept the unexpected consequences of his power, at the time when the enemy is no longer considered as an operational threat with the ability to inflict losses.

In fact, the Army seems then to be engaged in a process of denial about the realities of war and combat, a denial which plays into the hands of the Air Force and its self-promotional operation. By refusing to recognize these realities, the Army also refuses its own sacrificial heroism, which was pushed to the fore in *Glory* in 1990.

## 'Saving Ground Combat'

It is cinema that will come to the Army's rescue to get out of this impasse. Steven Spielberg's film of 1998 *Saving Private Ryan*, starring Tom Hanks and Matt Damon, is a revelation. It involves a commando unit who, just after the Normandy landings, are ordered to rescue a Private Ryan, the last survivor of a family of four brothers, three of whom have been killed in the same assault and in the Pacific. General Marshall himself decides to save this young man, at the cost of putting his entire section in danger, crossing war-torn Normandy and holding a town to the death against a German offensive.

This film caused a tremendous collective shock in the United States! The first signs of it were cases of fainting and panic attacks among veterans in American cinemas when the film was shown. The Pentagon had to set up a phone number and psychological helpline to respond to the thousands of calls from men who had never been able to speak on their return to the United States about the suffering and distress they had endused and that the film had reawakened. The star of the film, Tom Hanks, even became head of a fund-raising organization to create a memorial to these soldiers.

These collective phenomena were triggered by the combat scenes sequence. The landing in Normandy is an astonishing spectacle, filmed on the shoulder by following the advance of American troops caught in the 'grinder' of German defences. The fighting is shown with a rawness unequalled since Sam Peckinpah, provoking distress, a sense of urgency and stifling claustrophobia.

Steven Spielberg was inspired by long discussions with Samuel Fuller, who took part in the landings as a military film made and declared that the only way to capture the violence of the experience would be to open fire in the cinema at the same time. What is more, Spielberg got information on the latest research in military sociology and in the sociology of war and combat. He made his film a study on the reality of the soldier at war. The commando unit is filmed in two ways: conventionally in one sense with episodes of rough fraternity between soldiers, in the tradition of American war films, and a naturalistic documentary on a 'primary group', that is a small social circle created by the common experience of men at war who lived cheek by jowl for long enough to know that training, communal life and fighting are woven with extremely strong threads of solidarity. These primary groups ensure the cohesion of armies.

The primary group of commandos, a special forces unit specialized in missions of infiltration, preparation and those at the vanguard of offensives, fluctuates between the system of values that comes from their life in civvy street and the 'brutalization process' to which it is subjected. Brutalization, a gradual transformation of the soldiers system of values so that they adapt to the fragility of their life and that of their adversaries, forces them to adopt the behaviour of deadly violence, which becomes the norm.

One sequence illustrates this development particularly well: it concerns the scene where the soldiers begin laughing and playing 'Happy Families' with the dog tags of dead soldiers whilst the young recruits going up to the firing line pass by. Yet Steven Spielberg does not dare to take this to its conclusion; he makes the characters have a conventional dialogue, in a formal tone, about their mothers who miss them or their first girlfriends.

The final battle is a peak of extreme military violence: again, the director follows the logic described in combat studies, which demonstrates that urban warfare is the worst of all because of the scattering of forces inside the urban landscape and the useless individual engagements between soldiers, where the removal of critical distances means that there is no other way out for individuals than by the death of their adversary. The scene where the SS soldier and a Jewish American soldier fight each other with fists and knives while one ends up cutting the other's throat, begging him to leave him alone so it can all end, depicts a very rarely spoken, and even less shown, truth.

This level of unique realism provoked a realization in the midst of the military command: the soldiers discovered that Hollywood studios had improved simulation techniques to a level superior to theirs. There followed an increase in in-depth contact between the studios, the Army and the Navy throughout 1998 and 1999. The studios then committed themselves to improving training and simulation techniques, which soldiers first of all study then use, before handing them back to the studios who can use them to make films. These arrangements involved contracts rising to tens of millions of dollars.

From then on, military testimony combined to recognize that the conditioning of recruits does not stop developing, particularly with regard to the psychological preparation for close combat. At the same time, the quality of combat scenes followed the same curve of progression in the cinema, as actor lives became less and less easy. On the set of *Saving Private Ryan*, Tom Hanks and his colleagues had to live in character to the point where successive incidents of exhaustion and bouts of gastro-enteritis reminded everyone that professional actors are not elite soldiers and have to be in one piece at the end of filming. In 2002, a marine corps officer declared that the simulations perfected in Hollywood allowed soldiers to learn to kill more easily by imagining they were in a film.

The year 1998 was thus one of the advent of military sociology in cinema, but also war coming back to earth, something which was desired jointly by the Army, the Navy and Hollywood, in order to respond to the biting challenge launched by the Air Force and *space power* to the other pillars of the defence and security establishment. If the reaction of the Army was support for *Private Ryan*, the Navy was happy with Ridley Scott's *GI Jane*, starring Demi Moore and Viggo Mortensen.

A female Naval communications officer signs up for the Navy Seals corps selection procedure against a backdrop of a programme of integrating women into the armed forces. After refusing to have the category 'female' applied to her, she manages to be accepted into the Seals, painfully and despite a fierce campaign of belittlement. The film ends with a mission to rescue Rangers (therefore from the Army) on a special operation off the Libyan coast, during which she takes charge of the unit and saves their deputy from the Libyans.

The filming highlights preparations for the specific area of of 'littoral warfare' and the ability to land and pick up elite Navy troops. In addition, that the final combat takes place in Libya is not a chance occurrence of the script: Libya figures in the list of 'rogue states' set out in 1996 by the Pentagon, including Iraq, Iran, Sudan, Afghanistan and North Korea. The list is added to or reduced at will, depending on relations between Washington and these countries, and the circumstances of the endlessly fluctuating power relations between the State Department, the CIA, the Pentagon and the White House.

By showing special forces intervening on the Libyan coast, Ridley Scott supports the Navy's official claim of declaring itself the only one in a position to ensure the siege or potential encirclement of rogue states from the sea, thanks to the permanent presence of its fleet on every ocean of the world. It thus claims a geo-strategic role of which the Air Force is incapable. What is more, this strategic dimension is increased by the assertion that the Navy is the new *melting pot* and the realization of the American ideal of equality. The Navy allows the integration of black people, Latinos, poor white people and women, giving to them a common identity and legitimizing their sense of belonging to the American nation. (It is moreover interesting to make the connection between this and the Pentagon's promise in September 2003 that young people of foreign descent will be naturalized if they sign up for the armed forces.) Through this film, the Navy becomes the symbol of the realization of American political ideals and the strategic ideal of global security.

However, Ridley Scott's choices in filming unconsciously reveal the undifferentiated 'rag bag' character of the famous doctrine of 'rogue states' (or those designated as such). The fighting takes place not against clearly-defined and individualized Libyan soldiers but against silhouettes, essentially seen with their backs to the sun and their Bedouin headdresses easily distinguishable from the port. In contrast, the American soldiers are highly individualized by the filming, and are thrown into the nightmare of meeting the 'Other', who is inevitably hostile.

It must be noted that this interpretation of American doctrine according to the standard of the Frontier does not take into account the fact that the coastal intervention breaches territorial sovereignty. The enemy is, in this case, Libyan but could be anyone. Libya is dangerous, however, since it is one of the so-called rogue states, and as such is a legitimate target for distruction. The way to enemy is presented is totally at odds, for example, with the systematic humanization of German soldiers in the war films of the 1960s and 1970s, which accompanied the process of Germany integration into NATO.

Ridley Scott's film thus defines the implicit category in American thought of a 'Third World enemy', who does not deserve any respect and whose rights are, by definition, non-existent, since it is *a priori* built and perceived as a threat. In the same way, the cohesion of American society ensured by belonging to elite Navy forces is reinforced by it.

## Fighting Nature

The issue of ground combat poses a larger question than the one about material strategic relations between the United States and those they identify as threats: that of their relationship with Nature. In effect, a strategic threat is not simply an armed entity refusing to accept American hegemony, but all forms of power that make American society vulnerable or put it in danger. The uncontrollable manifestations of Nature thus appear as strategic threats because of their capacity to endanger the material framework of society.

In this way, when *Independence Day*, *GI Jane* and *Saving Private Ryan* were filmed or distributed, Nature was perceived as dangerous just as much in Hollywood as in the different centres of strategic research, official or private. The effects of global warming, pollution, the disappearance of types of animal life, or the anxiety generated by the series of weaknesses in the Californian subsoil began to be studied from a strategic point view.

*Volcano* (1997), by Mick Jackson, starring Tommy Lee Jones, bears witness to this presence of the environment as a strategic fear. The action starts off with an 'ecological Pearl Harbor' in Los Angeles, where a volcano erupts in the middle of the city. Within minutes, an enormous flow of lava builds up and begins flowing down the streets, threatening to burn everything in its wake. The head of environmental emergencies in the area takes charge of things, coordinates fire crews, police, road workers and the national guard and organizes the digging of a breach towards the sewers in order to direct the lava in towards the sea after channelling it by the building a barrier.

This pseudo-disaster movie is a true national security film where the invader is none other than Nature herself, who threatens to destroy human society and whose advancing tide is only kept in check after a fierce struggle on the ground: in the film's main scene, the fire crews form a wall of water hoses behind a rampart of cement blocks and wait for the advance of the lava, supported by a fleet of helicopters laden with water.

## Drift

If ground combat is still deemed necessary, it is still frightening. The spectacular and tragic aspect of this type of combat is appreciated by Hollywood, who find in it an important source of scripts and guaranteed success. But, in the very specific domain of national security, the major studios cannot allow themselves to favour one point of view over another. Promoting the Army and the Navy has an opposite effect, represented in the possible drift linked to the use of military ground force, which is undoubtedly necessary for achieving victory, but whose potential for violence and massacre is not ethically acceptable for American society.

This ambivalence dates back to the splits in American society during the Vietnam War, where a deep-seated mistrust resulted in respect of soldiers actions. Reworked by the 'clinical war' in the Gulf, this recollection and the collective sentiments that ensue result in the belief that the United States is from now on militarily invincible, in whatever situation, and that any enemy can only be swept aside. The problem therefore becomes one of regulating the use of power and developing the military ethic of an army which can no longer be beaten. Hollywood reacts to the dangerous ultra-powerful Nature of the Army in *Three Kings* (1999), followed by *Rules of Engagement* (2000).

David O. Russell's *Three Kings*, starring George Clooney, begins during the last hours of the Gulf War. Two non-commissioned officers, a Delta Force officer and a trooper set up a private club after finding a card indicating the site of an enormous cache of gold in Iraqi territory, while American troops are across the border. They chance their arm, get the gold but then witness the repression of the local Shi'ite population by Saddam Hussein's army. The team leader intervenes and the four Americans find themselves unwittingly in charge of a Shi'ite population who believe they have come to liberate them.

The whole film follows the trials of these 'three kings' who wander in the desert with these refugees in order to get them into Iran. They end up securing the help of a US-French squadron from the coalition by offering to share the loot. They transport the Shi'ite people to the Iranian border and watch them cross, each one of them wondering what fate lies in store for the unfortunate wretches. The Americans then go home, one becomes a military adviser in Hollywood, the other the contented director of a carpet store.

*Three Kings* portrays American difficulties in assuming victory on the ground. The first sequences show the GIs, pleased at having won and treating the Iraqi prisoners as 'sand niggers', but not comprehending the reason for their own presence in Kuwait.

To find a reason, they begin this treasure hunt which results in their troubled realisation of the consequences of American strategy and a military victory without a clearly pre-established political goal, other than one of leaving Saddam Hussein the means with which to control Iraq while chasing him out of Kuwait. This military ground victory becomes a tragedy for the civilian population, who believed they had been liberated, but in fact had been abandoned to the savage repression of the Iraqi regime. The ability to achieve victories on the ground thus increases the question of their significance, in relation to the value system professed by the United States.

This questioning is exacerbated in William Friedkin's *Rules of Engagement* (2000), starring Tommy Lee Jones and Samuel L. Jackson. The American ambassador to Yemen is besieged by a hostile crowd, and a marine commando unit is sent from the aircraft carrier of the Sixth Fleet. American personnel are evacuated then the commando captain fires on the crowd. Twenty-four people die and countless dozens are injured. The captain is court-martialed. The tribunal panel tries to get him jailed to avoid creating anti-American feeling in the Arab world and internationally, but his lawyer gets him acquitted by arguing that he respected the 'rules of engagement', having had to respond to gunfire.

*Rules of Engagement* depicts the possible drift in military ground force during combat at a time when war takes place in the Third World. The boundary between war and social control tends then to become blurred, posing the question of the legitimacy of using American fire power, which is totally disproportionate to that of the enemy. The film finds the solution by erasing the difference between civilians and combatants, the carrying of weapons being their lowest common denominator, hence the possibility of 'firing into the crowd' without that notion being challenged; by this proposition, the film is actively engaged in the American rehabilitation of ground combat which has been under way for several years.

Hollywood's involvement in the area of combat and its doctrines, but also its drift, are useful to the Army, but cause a certain amount of trouble, seen in a *Strategic Review* article in June 2000 when an Army lieutenant-colonel declares that at the time when William Friedkin's film was being shown in American cinemas, ground combat was very controlled and 'is no longer the chaos depicted by *Saving Private Ryan* or *The Empire Strikes Back*'.

In addition, this issue is complicated by the entire American strategic culture, distinguished by the choice of absolute superiority on the logistical level and of fire-power in order to obtain an indisputable result as quickly as possible. This culture explains the interest felt in respect of air power and the sense of impatience towards ground operations and the numerous drifts they can lead to, the 'unfortunate mistakes' against civilians which sometimes blot the copybook of victory.

Hence all the ambiguities of this film: it demonstrates the impossibility for Americans of not achieving a victory on the ground, and the political problems that this invulnerability can cause, but also the status for the least vulnerable civilian. Furthermore, William Friedkin tackles here a problem carefully set aside by Steven Spielberg, who develops his soldiers in a Normandy absolutely empty of any French presence, save a very quick sequence involving a family – who are then quickly forgotten.

On the other hand, the demonstration of this near invincibility of the American army on the collective level 'forgets' the ideology of 'zero losses'. This ideal is replaced by that of losses so reduced that they become insignificant as much on the tactical as the political level. To do this, logistical superiority is applied to individual soldiers. But if viewing marines equipped with armour and conventional weapons of terrifying capability is not shocking insofar as they save American civilians in a film, things take another turn when they retain them on peace missions in the real world.

This is the case with US marines based in Kosovo since 1999, nicknamed 'ninja turtles' by the other members of the international force because they never go out of their entrenched position with their combat gear, in an environment controlled, among others, by French gendarmes on bicycles. That above all implies that these marines consider the place where peace is being brought to as a combat zone where everyone can be an armed and dangerous enemy and from whom they must be able to protect themselves, even by killing them. Just like in the movies.

In addition, commandos caught in the wasp's nest of Mogadishu in October 1993 all attest to a feeling of incredulity, due to the impression of 'being in a film', and have difficulty admitting that what was taking place really was happening to them. Their reaction is massive recourse to fire power, which left, at the very least, a thousand victims from the civilian population, as well as combatants.

This drift, which is a potential warning sign for the marines in Kosovo, reveals to what extent the American system does not consider the world according to experience but according to *a priori* ideologies and images that sustain each another, whilst practical experience continues to pose problems in order to be integrated into the doctrines of combat.

Nevertheless, while the Air Force and *space power* are promoted, fundamental and strategic tools in the globalization era, cinema, backed by military research, reminds us that American strategy cannot do without ground interventions. Put 'simply', ground combat is considered fraught with the potential for drift, and these considerations all converge during the period from 2000 to 2003.

# 8

# AROUND SEPTEMBER 11

The attacks of 11 September 2001 had unexpected effects on relations between the production of strategy and national security cinema. The towers in Manhattan collapsed and the Pentagon went up in flames, shattering the American myth of US soil being a sanctuary. The collective trauma it represented must be assessed from the origins of this myth and that of the system which cultivated and maintained it. The events of 11 September simultaneously attacked American society, its national security system, the way the United States portrayed itself and the whole country's strategic culture.

## Tensions

When this strategic culture is polarized around the 'idea' of a relatively well-defined outside threat, it is able to become the bulwark of national consensus. But the belligerence of the 11 September attacks, coming from outside the US, was difficult to take in because of its originality and cognitive dissonance, that is the discrepancy between the ideas in themselves and the actual experience. This difficulty is shown in the great tension between Hollywood's traditional tendency to 'join forces' with Washington and support the prevailing ideology in a time of crisis, and an inclination to distance themselves by refusing simplistic discourse on the event.

In fact, tensions were already in existence; they did not suddenly emerge in the brutality of the event, but were in evidence from 2000 with the immense success of Ridley Scott's *Gladiator*, starring Russell Crowe. The emperor Marcus Aurelius asks the valiant Spanish centurion Maximus to be his successor. Marcus Aurelius is then killed by his son Commodus, who becomes emperor. Maximus becomes a slave after his family is massacred, then a gladiator, and his reputation is soon such that he threatens the popularity and legitimacy of Commodus. They confront each other in the arena in man-to-man combat and both die, the senators taking advantage of their deaths to claim power.

This film is a political event in itself insofar as its subject is that of the legitimacy of empire. 'The world is the darkness, Rome is the light', says Maximus, after his legions have beaten the Germanic Barbarians at the furthest reaches of the Empire. It thus reprises the historic American mythological idea of the United States as City upon a Hill, whose light illuminates the world, justifying a large-scale military expedition 'to the margins'.

However, this military-ideological aim is complicated to a great extent. Commodus kills his father in order to inherit the empire and challenge the senators, who are looking for military support, whilst the new emperor is feted by the masses because of a significant policy of 'bread and games'. Political legitimacy appears then to become elusive: senators are inclined above all to wherever power lies, the masses are nothing other than consumerist and capricious, emperors are exhausted or demented while military power is dangerous. This tragic circularity makes a hopeless spectacle of imperial power, because it can only be arbitrary and dangerous.

Ridley Scott shows in this way that, with heroism and military superiority projected across the entire globe, political forces are at work which have nothing to do with the glorious ideology conveyed by the imperial argument which justifies its grip on the outside world. On the other hand, the real life of the State is a perpetual war between factions that use public opinion and the armed forces as instruments. Above all, *Gladiator* is a deeply pessimistic film where the only hope of a happy life rests in the removal of power, particularly when it is directionless and the counter-balances to it no longer fulfil their function.

This runaway success of summer 2000 also revealed the existence of fracture lines between the Hollywood *establishment* and the national security system, as the filming in the same year of Clint Eastwood's *Space Cowboys* equally demonstrated. Blockbusters with political and strategic ideas no longer reflected the prevailing concepts at the heart of the strategic debate; they questioned the structures and legitimacy of it. In fact, at the end of the Clinton era, Hollywood often took it upon itself to doubt Washington and the legitimacy of American power, because of the way it was being used and going against the sacred and fundamental principles that founded US civilization.

These doubts provided the material for the great success of summer 2001 – *Swordfish*, by Dominic Sena, starring John Travolta and Halle Berry. The shadowy head of a clandestine organization hires a genius computer hacker to create a computer virus that will be used to divert colossal sums of drug trafficking money which has been confiscated by the Drug Enforcement Agency. In fact, this money is destined to finance the activities of the FBI's 'Black Cell', which is ordered to engage in terrorist activities against 'America's enemies'. Black Cell is controlled by a member of the Senate Commission on intelligence activities until he tries to abolish it – which is a fatal mistake. The extremely violent and illegal activities of the cell are justified by the idea of 'protecting the American way', even at the cost of innocent lives, so the 'enemies' are killed.

The film ends with a spectacular hold-up: bank customers are taken hostage and transformed into human bombs and the terrorists disappear in the confusion. The last sequence shows them re-emerging under a new disguise and using their funds to blow up a ship carrying an Arab terrorist leader.

This extremely rich and ambiguous film is a veritable inventory of the problems posed by the strategy of asymmetric warfare, which was put in place to fight the terrorist threat, and by the 'auto-asymmetricisation' of the American strategic system, which consists of setting up coercive teams and networks organized along terrorist lines in order to fight their 'counterparts' who are looking to slip through the American security net. To this end, members of US security networks require the same levels of motivation and fanaticism as their adversaries in their reprisals, repression and deterrent operations.

The film thus States in explicit fashion the relationship between the end and the means. Is protecting the 'American way' worth criminalizing a section of the national security system outside of any clearly-defined State of war? Which vision of the world is the most legitimate? Which is the most 'realistic'? Are the two notions inextricably linked? And if so, in what way? In the words of the *faux* cynic who leads Black Cell and is genuinely and acutely involved in his secret war against the 'enemies of America', 'We are at war, even if you can't see it!'

For this reason, he considers it legitimate to engage in the same practices on the inside as he fights against on the outside, even if that involves maintaining a global war, which, after being persuaded to wage a just war, is the crucible of the threats against which he has dedicated his life to eradicating. However, the film is completely clear on the fact that the self-criminalization of a branch of the secret services can only have violent repercussions on American society, and pose radical questions about its system of values. In fact, this particularly shadowy aspect of national security ends up inspiring as much fear as the terrorists, as much at the FBI as with officials and audiences. It is in this context that the attacks of 11 September took place one month later.

## The Test of Reality

The terrorist destruction of the twin towers in Manhattan and the Pentagon in Washington was an event of rare complexity that escaped all simplistic rhetoric. Whilst, since the Gulf War, the strategic system had been continually increasing its power through developing technology, it was put in check by unsophisticated and home-made means. It involved the practical application of the theory defined by American strategists since 1997 about asymmetric warfare, the war waged by America's enemies who infiltrate and act upon the weaknesses of power.

The attacks of 11 September caused an immense shock because, for the first time since the Anglo-American war of 1812, they symbolized the end of the inviolable Nature of American soil. In addition, for the first time since 1945, a threat, whose development mobilized the US strategy production industry and the cinema industry, was actually borne out in reality.

The destruction of the twin towers in New York, before being seen live on television, had been filmed a certain number of times by the cinema, or described in science-fiction novels, spy thrillers or political fiction. In the 1950s, extraterrestrials regularly destroyed New York, a destruction evoked again at the end of *Planet of the Apes* (1968) and, in 1979, in Roland Neame's *Meteor*, with Sean Connery, where a giant meteor destroys the two towers before disappearing into the Manhattan earth. This destruction is taken up again in 1996 by the extraterrestrials of *Independence Day*, then, in 1998, both in *Deep Impact* and *Armageddon*.

In literature, the idea of a devastating terrorist attack is at the centre of the intrigue of Mario Puzo's *The Fourth K* (1989), where a mini atomic bomb explodes in Manhattan. In *State of Siege* (1990) by Stephen Coonts, a series of large-scale terrorist attacks are launched by Colombian cartels in Washington, against Congress, the White House and the Pentagon. One of the most impressive of these literary fictions is that developed by Tom Clancy in *Debt of Honour* (1995). This book follows the escalation of a commercial dispute between Japan and the United States into a real war, which the Americans win within days by employing asymmetric techniques (terrorist commandos in Tokyo, new, ultra-precise weapons, the infiltration of special forces into Japanese territory) and conventional methods (air assaults). In order to avenge the death of his fighter-pilot brother, a civilian airline pilot crashes his 747 into Congress just as the President is giving a televised address.

This imagined American concept of catastrophe and national security, which replays Pearl Harbor on a loop by regularly condemning two of the three landmark US cities (New York, Washington and Los Angeles), dates back at least to the beginning of the 1950s, even to the start of the twentieth century. It is reflected in the entire production of literary and cinematic fiction resulting out of the awareness of new threats, which are often used by the cultural and media *civil defence* organizations. This fiction injected a collective feeling of imminent war-like catastrophe into the American mental universe for nearly 20 years. From the 1970s and 1980s, an even greater number of thriller writers and authors of political and geo-strategy fiction emerged from the different sub-communities of national security. These three genres were very much in vogue in the United States and the most successful of them could sell hundreds of thousands of copies. Stephen Coonts is a former fighter pilot and high-ranking Air Force officer; Tom Clancy, who still maintains very close links with the CIA, became a lobbyist for the Pentagon and the Republican party; and as well as writing the *Godfather*, Mario Puzo is a specialist in organized crime.

But, until 11 September 2001, these literary and cinematic depictions of threat did little more than create a distance between the perception of reality and that of threat. They set up a fictional barrier between the public and its fears, which was largely sustained by literary make-believe. In just a few hours, the 11 September attacks broke down this barrier by forcing the test of reality onto this imaginary world. In front of their television screens, the community of citizens (including those in national security) went from being spectators removed from events to spectators and citizens involved in the reality and demonstration of their fear. The threat, having become real, forced a reconsideration of the strategic imagination: having been viewed as the harbinger of 11 September, it lost part of its ability to produce distance.

The symbolic shock was immense. In order for its significance to be taken on board, the media and political system responded within hours by making reaction to the attacks the exhibition of a national call-to-arms. The images of New York and the Pentagon rapidly became those principally of dust and bodies hidden by sheets or American flags.

This refusal to show blood was both a fundamental aesthetic and political choice, which had already been used months before in Michael Bay's *Pearl Harbor*, where the destruction of the base, the fighting and the massacres are depicted without blood being shown on screen. This approach is adopted by the media in the days that followed 11 September in order to symbolize an event that had no parallel in American strategic recall other than in fiction.

This borrowing by news television of procedures that had been thoroughly tested in the cinema was spontaneous. This can be ascertained by the contrasting way in which the attacks in Bali of autumn 2002 were covered by the American media: this time, they highlighted the bloody dimension of the event and the horror of the population. But the attack did not take place on US soil, and the victims were Indonesian and Australian, not American. The fact that there was no blood in the images of 11 September clearly signified: if the nation is not bleeding, it is neither wounded nor mortal.

This choice orientated the possible public perception of the size of the 11 September attacks in decisive fashion. This method followed films and novels that invoked catastrophe in order to better use catharsis and project it within minutes of the event via the enormous media machine in the form of a spectacle into offices, living rooms, kitchens, bathrooms, in other words into the professional and personal heart of American society. Most activities were interrupted on 11 September and caused a strong surge in emotions, experienced individually, because of the Nature of the media, and collectively, because of the sentiment of national belonging.

However, the repeated showing of the attacks created something new in the history of the world's media: for several days, by following precise cinematic codes, broadcast news depicted a strategic shift of an importance unequalled anywhere except in films, hence the flood of testimony from people declaring to have had a feeling of unreality, the impression of 'being in a film'.

This feeling of time-lag was accentuated by the real effects of repeating the event on television. In effect, millions of Americans were directly affected by the attack. In the hours that followed, all aeroplanes in American airspace had to land at the nearest airport, which disrupted the lives of millions of people. At the same time, in most cities, skyscrapers were evacuated so as not to risk another tragedy.

This gigantic movement of population made those who were caught up in the situation potential victims in a State of imminent death and led them to share the experience of fear as well as a feeling of vulnerability that transformed the urban landscape into a trap; until then, the urban landscape had been the vertical illustration of the success of the most modern and attractive civilization in the world. The rest of the American population found itself a spectator of this same drama.

For every citizen affected, the expression of the terrorist moment in real time conferred a real presence on the idea of the omnipresence of the terrorist threat. This led to a narcissistic wound at the national level, perfectly expressed by the president George W. Bush during his address to the nation on 15 September: 'Who would want to attack us while we are so good?' He expressed in this way the feeling of collective suffering of every community who were victims of such an attack. This was exacerbated further by the American certainty that the legitimacy deriving from their particular status among nations should make it unthinkable to even imagine attacking them, unless they were an ally of evil.

In this sense, the means found by the political system to absorb the shock was creating the discourse on the fight of Good against Evil in an atmosphere of military mobilisation.

## Does Hollywood Go to War?

It is against this backdrop that a meeting was held in Hollywood on 11 November 2001 between representatives of the major studios, the head of the actors union, the powerful and redoubtable Jack Valenti, and Karl Rove, President George W Bush's eminent political adviser. The aim of the meeting was the coordination of American foreign policy, dominated by the 'war against terrorism', with Hollywood productions.

Karl Rove insisted on the administration's desire to avoid any propaganda and stressed the need for 'clear and honest' information. In addition, he implored Hollywood producers and directors not to dramatize the 'war against terrorism' on screen by following the famous Huntington model of the 'war of civilizations'. He reiterated what has become the Bush administration's mantra since the start of the fight against the Taliban in Afghanistan, and oft repeated by the president: 'This is not a war against Islam nor against Muslims but a war against terrorism!' On the other hand, the discussion also very much centred on the need to promote a good image of the integration of American Muslims into American society. (We could moreover assume the emergence of a new genre of supporting roles in national security films, played by 'good' Muslims, dying in order to get rid of the threat!)

This meeting between Karl Rove and Jack Valenti corresponded to a major political shift between the American power bases. Whilst in 1942, President Roosevelt had summoned the most eminent Hollywood producers and directors to the White House in order to unhesitatingly assign them their role in the national call-to-arms, in 2001 the all-powerful presidential political adviser had to make the trip to Hollywood to meet Lyndon B. Johnson's former political adviser, who had become head of the Motion Pictures Association, following a certain number of powerful people, including Ronald Reagan.

What is more, Hollywood has, politically, a traditionally more Democratic than Republican sensibility in the area of national security, as is seen in the adaptations of Tom Clancy novels, among others, while the Bush administration is, in numerous respects, a 'hard-line' reincarnation of the Reagan administration.

Also, behind the apparent consensus established by this meeting, its very appearance revealed the reciprocal malaise and mistrust in relation to the question of 11 September. The enormity of the event was such that political power had to ensure minimal regulation of its treatment by cinema and not allow itself the slightest *faux pas* whilst the war in Afghanistan was under way, in a context of increasing tensions with Muslim countries. On the other hand, the power of cinema had reached such a level that it was no longer as controllable as it once was, but it could not allow itself to alienate the public (by going against the consensus forged by the attacks, which had established support for the positions of the Bush administration) nor, in a wider sense, State power and its potential for reprisals .

This prudence was the basis for the decision to put back the release of two major productions on the theme of terrorism, *The Sum of All Fears* (2001), by Phil Alden Robinson, and *Collateral Damage* (2001), by Andrew Davis. These two films, produced and filmed at the end of the Clinton era, thus before the attacks, became very sensitive political subjects because of the inability, as much of the specialists in public opinion at the White House as the marketing executives at the major studios, to gauge the reactions of the public.

Also, the story of the production and distribution of *The Sum of All Fears* became one of the automatic adjustment of a major studio to the current international strategic climate, to which the political power had to adapt, and not the other way around. The film was initially another adaptation of a Tom Clancy novel that envisages the acquisition by Palestinian extremists of an Israeli nuclear bomb at a time when America has managed to bring peace on the Middle East, including Turkey and Greece; they transform it into a micro-bomb and explode it in Denver on Superbowl Sunday. The American president, believing it to be a Russian attack, wants to launch a nuclear strike on the Russian Federation but he is prevented from doing so by the deputy director of the CIA, Jack Ryan. Not long afterwards, the terrorists are killed, and Ryan becomes the director of the CIA. As usual in the works of Tom Clancy, the novel is full of Republican ideology; he promotes out-and-out unilateralism, reflects the shared, right-wing views of the Republican party and the Israeli hawks on the Middle East, while portraying the United States above all as a benevolent power because it brings peace to the world.

Notified about this project, the Washington-based lobby group the Council on American-Arab Relations (CAIR), was concerned; they effectively feared that, as in the book, the film gave a bad image of Islam and Muslims. Having contacted the studio, the CAIR learned that the script had been changed: the Arab and Islamic terrorists had become European neo-Nazis who are looking to provoke Russia and the United States into destroying each other.

The director, Phil Alden Robinson, wrote to the CAIR in person: 'I hope you will be reassured that I have no intention of promoting negative images of Muslims or Arabs and I wish you the best in your continuing efforts to combat discrimination'. Omar Ahmad, board chairman of the CAIR, replied: 'Given the existing prejudice against and stereotyping of Islam and Muslims, we believe this film could have had a negative impact on the lives of ordinary American Muslims, particularly children. We are pleased that Mr Robinson took the initiative to help eliminate religious and ethnic bias from his film. This move should set a precedent for other movie producers.' The film's release, initially scheduled for November 2001, was put back to the start of July 2002.

The release was arranged like a political and media event: it was welcomed from Moscow by Dick Cheney, the powerful American vice-president on a visit to President Putin, and from Washington by President Bush himself. Because of its cinematic qualities, it was the hit of summer 2002.

The script becomes the story of criminal Russian experts making a home-made nuclear bomb from an Israeli nuclear device for a group of European neo-Nazis, all against a backdrop of international Russian-American tension. The bomb explodes in Baltimore, the president of the United States rapidly loses control of himself and his team whilst the Russian military command is on the brink of panic. The situation is saved by Jack Ryan, a young CIA analyst, who diffuses the tension by discovering the plot with the help of a 'mole' in the Kremlin.

The film ends on an astonishing scene: whilst the official ceremonies are taking place, Jack Ryan and his girlfriend are picnicking on the grass of the Mall, their backs turned to the White House, where a bilateral accord on disarmament is being signed concerning arsenals of weapons of mass destruction. The Russian presidential adviser appears. An old and redoubtable general, he is also the mole who has helped avoid nuclear war. He suggests Jack Ryan becomes his pen-friend, like his 'old friend', the director of the CIA, who was killed in the attack. Ryan accepts, and the old general offers him and his girlfriend a wedding gift. The last shot is that of this old spy and shadowy Russian political adviser walking away in the direction of the obelisk, the Egyptian symbol of freemasonry and wisdom.

The *Sum of All Fears* is a work of great depth, where terrorism is treated according to a singular philosophy of international relations. The film highlights the need for State-to-State communication and cooperation, which could be the work of a 'caste', both of State and meta-state control, capable of injecting the necessary wisdom into controlling the increase in violence in international relations. In the film, terrorism becomes not only the emergence of evil, but also a particular form of political pathology, coming from Europe. The film also lets it be understood that Nazism has not been completely destroyed by the American-Soviet alliance in World War Two and the two superpowers, the rich and the poor, have to keep a watchful and coercive eye again on European politics. Europe is seen as a centre of international subversion where a trans-nationalized Neo-nazism is growing and whose ability to act extends to Russia, the United States and the Middle East. In order to reign in Europe, it is in the United States and Russia's interests to collaborate, by forming a system of strategic relations where Washington has to acknowledge the autonomous political and strategic capacity of Moscow, and are themselves forced to recognize the relativity of their power: they are not a 'solitary superpower' contrary to what Samuel Huntington has written.

This film thus conveys a neo-realist philosophy of international relations that takes into account the reality of the State of power on the international stage, by injecting it with the inherited wisdom of the States of the Old World, as much to avert certain terrorist outrages as to oblige American political and strategic leaders to balance their actions and reactions.

*The Sum of All Fears* is an important film as well because it shows the explosion of the nuclear micro-bomb in Baltimore. This scene is short, sparing and effective: the bomb site is 'flattened' and the town is covered in dust.

The firefighters, police and doctors are heroic, but the many injured do not bleed. Realistic scenes, which have already been seen on television, are thus magnified through a cinematic discourse that gives sense to the images of the 'massive' danger to American society, yet were filmed before the televised repeats of the attacks on New York. What is more, by recalling that, in actual fact, international relations are always dominated by the nuclear balance between Russia and the United States, paradoxically, the film is reassuring, reintegrating the American strategic situation into a history and tradition, thus in normality.

Finally, we can find in this work a sophisticated, strongly anti-Republican comment on the Nature and origin of the American relationship with terrorism: in this way, in the hours that follow the attack, specialists from the Strategic Command discover that the plutonium for the bomb was stolen from an American nuclear power station in 1969. The Kremlin mole tells Jack Ryan that this plutonium was stolen by the CIA in order to be given illegally to the Israelis, who were in the middle of developing their nuclear military programme.

There is here a very precise allusion to, even an accusation about, American foreign policy under Richard Nixon and Henry Kissinger between 1968 and 1973: this policy is allegedly the technological and geo-political crucible of contemporary strategic threats; the stress throughout the film is put on American strategic over-investment in the Middle East, whilst the 'real' threats could come from a little-known, dark and secretive Europe. Furthermore, the European political authorities could be concerned by what such a film reveals of Hollywood's future politics about its portrayal of Europe. In addition, the script was written between 1999 and 2000, in the midst of a Republican offensive, both politically – directly against President Clinton, through the Lewinsky affair – and strategically – by the revival in Congress of NMD budgets and programmes, which the film warns is of strictly no use in the event of a real ballistic offensive.

As with *Clear and Present Danger* (1994), the previous adaptation of a Tom Clancy novel, we have here a spy thriller that plays a part in Hollywood's falling out of line with the national security system when the latter is dominated by a hawkish, unilateralist, Republican establishment, this process being masked by the reprise of the prevailing and consensual theme of terrorism. But, undoubtedly, many political officials decrypted the signals sent out by Hollywood only too well, which explains the discretion exercised in political and security attempts to intervene directly.

On the other hand, if the message is hard-hitting against elected officials from the Republican party and their advisers, we witness here a rehabilitation of the CIA and its bureaucrats, who have been given a rough time by the press and the establishment since 1991, because they were accused, completely unjustifiably, of not having foreseen the invasion of Kuwait by Iraq. Throughout the whole film, Jack Ryan always gets the better of high-ranking officials who are incapable of listening to him, shut off as they are in their certainties. Furthermore, the production received a lot of help from the CIA, who opened up their buildings and provided a great deal of advice for the filming. This relationship illustrates the evolution in progress: the national security system ends up needing the major studios even more and being more dependent on them than the other way around.

This evolution is cemented by technological developments which give studios the means of recreating reality with digital special effects: the alignment between Hollywood and Washington is no longer a question of dependence but choice. In this way, when, in 1986 Tony Scott relied on the good will of the air forces of the Navy to film *Top Gun*, the aerial armada of the Air Force that sweeps out against the extraterrestrials of *Independence Day* was created by computers that reduced them down from models of F-16s. Hollywood's technological ability tips the balance of the interdependent relationship between national security productions and the national security State: the national security State, through the defence institutions' public relations offices in Hollywood, engages from now on in lobbying, to 'encourage' the adoption of one scenario or another, but strictly no longer has a determinant logistic authority on how a film turns out.

This distancing is even more acute in Tony Scott's *Spy Game* (2001), starring Robert Redford and Brad Pitt, which was also filmed before 11 September. By following the father-son relationship of a CIA recruitment agent and his 'protégé', the film retraces the activities of the Agency, from the end of the Vietnam War to 1991 via Libya. This account is one of the radicalization of agents, which ends with them having recourse to terrorism: in Libya, two agents organize an attack that kills 70 people in order to eliminate a Falangist chief. Finally, with the end of the Cold War and the opening up of commercial relations with the former Soviet Union and China, the Agency begins an internal purge to get rid of its very capable and troublesome *cold warriors*, at the risk of putting their lives in danger. They must then use their know-how to outsmart their own administration.

The film thus denounces the perversion of democratic values among the agents of the Cold War, which leads them to become executioners and terrorists in order to, ultimately, allow America to 'sell video recorders and washing machines to China'. *Spy Game* itself questions terrorism in dialectical terms: in effect, how to prevent the emergence of asymmetric terrorist enemies while American foreign policy justified similar practices in the previous 40 years.

*Spy Game* explicitly casts doubt on the legitimacy of American strategies, because they escape all democratic control and appeal to interests that have nothing to do with the ideals championed by the agents themselves. It establishes a clear distinction between agents who more or less support the horror of the actions in which they indulge, in the name of ideals that they refuse to question, and bureaucratic and political officials, who are able to turn their backs on what gave meaning to their actions during this time and become standard-bearers for the cynicism necessary for unbridled liberalism.

The complex Nature of the causes of terrorism is also examined in Andrew Davis *Collateral Damage*, with Arnold Schwarzenegger, which was supposed to be released on 14 September 2001 but was pushed back to spring 2002. Colombian extremists attack the FBI headquarters in Los Angeles. The 'collateral damage' is the death of the wife and son of a firefighter. The firefighter, exasperated by the dead-ends of the inquiry, disguises himself as a mechanic and leaves for Colombia, where he infiltrates a network of drug traffickers by looking after the upkeep of their agricultural machinery. He then discovers that the head of the narco-guerillas, who are responsible for the death of his family, is a former primary school teacher whose family was massacred during an offensive led by paramilitary troops of the CIA. The film ends when the FBI succeeds in preventing an attack in Washington, the Colombians being ready to kill a child in order to blow up the State Department, their own losses having plunged them into despair and hatred.

Again, an American film treats terrorism by refusing easy generalizations, underlining the responsibility of the United States whose unilateralist policy often facilitates the exploitation of the most deprived social groups and forces entire peasantries into armed revolt, terrorism and producing drugs. Terrorism is presented as the asymmetric effect of the trans-nationalization of the American national security system's indiscriminate and ultra-violent military practices. Through this film, and numerous others before it, the old rivalry between the CIA, which is only supposed to operate outside US soil, and the FBI, which is strictly in charge of internal security, sees the balance of power tip in favour of the FBI. From the mid-1990s, the FBI is the national security agency that competes with the CIA in the most effective manner, particularly by dealing with anti-terrorist investigations. What is more, the FBI does not suffer from the symbolic liabilities of nearly 50 years of 'clandestine operations' in the world, particularly in Latin America.

So, it is the films produced before 11 September that see themselves assigned the task of telling the story of the attacks and giving them meaning. On the political level, this meant that the studio executives considered them appropriate. They have not followed simple financial logic that requires a film to be profitable, because the major studios have had their own policy of self-censorship for 50 years: a film being only a product of its studio, it can just as well be radically re-shot as never distributed. This, for example, was the fate suffered by John McTiernan's *Rollerball* in 2001. The film was to have depicted a players revolt in an extremely violent televised sport, resulting in a Spartacus-like uprising. Seeming too sulphurous to producers, it nearly became a 'straight to video' movie, before being cut to pieces by a savage re-filming and a long sequence of meaningless fights.

This example illustrates to what extent the producers weighed up their decision in the distribution of *Spy Game*, *Collateral Damage* and *The Sum of All Fears*, topical films that distance themselves from the political and strategic powers when the latter appear to stray too far from the American tradition of consensus at the centre. In addition, the question of terrorism is too serious to be treated in a caricatured fashion in the style of the fight of good against evil, even if this rhetoric was beginning to supply the foreign policy discourse of the Bush administration. At the time when these films began to be distributed and to recommend a distanced and complex approach about these issues to the public, the strategic debate was filled with the concepts of 'pre-emptive war' and 'axis of evil'.

### 'We Were Soldiers'

On the strategic level, the period from the 11 September attacks to January 2002 was dominated by the military operation in Afghanistan and the fall of the Taliban. During the annual State of the Union address in January, President George W Bush set out the new American strategic doctrine of 'pre-emptive war'. This is defined less in relation to the existence of politically hostile regimes than military material, which are grouped together in the category of 'weapons of mass destruction'. This category of weapons groups together nuclear, chemical and biological weapons in indistinct fashion. Third World States that possess one or another of these weapons are accused implicitly of not respecting their aim as deterrents and wanting to use them. Against this dangerous, assumed irrationality, offensive warfare becomes effectively defensive and legitimate.

This idea of 'pre-emptive and just' war has been around since the Republican hawks came to power, the same people, moreover, who established the Strategic Defense Initiative under Ronald Reagan, or transformed Saddam Hussein into a strategic threat in 1990.

This pregnancy expresses itself from March 2002, in Randall Wallace's very ambiguous *We Were Soldiers*, starring Mel Gibson. Inspired by the autobiography of Lieutenant Colonel Harold Moore, this film evokes the terrible battle of La Drang Valley in Vietnam in 1965. Before the officer leaves for war, his eight-year-old daughter asks him what war is. He explains: 'Well, it is when people want to kill you, so you have to prevent them from doing so, by waging war!' This definition corresponds well to the idea of pre-emptive war: war is justified when, according to their own criteria, political and strategic officials identify what appears to them to be a hostile intention, whose possible consequences must be prevented.

Yet, at the same time, the rest of the film insists on the astuteness and heroism of the marines, and undermines the sense of this initial declaration. The film is certainly part of the movement that highlights ground combat as the means for victory, but, unlike *Saving Private Ryan*, *GI Jane* and *Glory*, the frightening intensity of the fighting regularly results in scenes of extremely crude horror. In addition, at the same time as the battle, the viewer follows the lives of the wives in their garrison town: day after day, one after another, they receive the letter announcing the death of their husband. This procedure gives the film-maker the means of putting the effects of the battle in the very heart of the American family. The battle does not only destroy soldiers, but society itself. The soldiers heroism also becomes that of their wives, but these two sides of the 'battle subject' only complement each other outwardly. In fact, the political meaning of the battle disappears as that of survival emerges.

This apparent promotion of pre-emptive war is finally completely confused by the last sequence: the night after the end of the battle, the Viet-Cong colonel is supervising the recovery of bodies, and, in front of the carnage, sighs, saying: 'Now they will believe we have won. They will come back until enough of them have been killed. There's enough for years!' Then, in tribute to the courage of American soldiers, he plants a small American flag on a tree branch, a salute analogous to that accorded during funeral services in a military cemetery. Furthermore, it is noteworthy that the director, Randall Wallace, is English, the very product of an ancient military and warring civilisation that does not shy away from the realities of war, and it is in this respect that he contrasts American concepts of war with its realities.

Also, at the time when the American strategic system is embarking on a campaign of justifying the war or wars by emphasizing their pre-emptive character, a major war film develops a discourse with two meanings. The valour of the soldiers is put forward but this valour is inversely proportionate to the wisdom of the strategic decision-makers, who are presented as bloated with arrogance when faced with the power that they can mobilize for a very badly worked-out cause, which leads American soldiers, their officials, families, the Viet-Cong and their families to catastrophe.

However, this double-edged cinematic discourse does not cut across the whole of Hollywood. The nationalistic and militaristic camp was undergoing a spectacular revival from the end of the 1990s, which is condensed in the production of *Black Hawk Down*, which was filmed at the same time as *We Were Soldiers*.

*Black Hawk Down* (2001) is the adaptation of journalist Mark Bowden's best-seller. It is a minutely-detailed inquiry into the catastrophic attempt to arrest General Aidid in Mogadishu in October 1993. The book follows the evolution of events from the perspective of American special forces, Somalian fighters and the civilian population. It sheds light on the radical difference in the philosophy of war between the Americans, who have recourse to a formidable technological superiority to stay alive, find themselves dependent on it and are slow to adapt, and the Somalians, who are prepared to die in combat and who have recognised the infinite reticence of the Americans to make this sacrifice.

The author's talent has made this book a contemporary classic of military history, to the extent that Mark Bowden is regularly invited to give conferences and seminars in the most prestigious research centres and military academies.

But Ridley Scott and his scriptwriter choose to go against the spirit of the book by producing a film that only see things from the point of view of American soldiers caught up in an urban battle in the depths of the Third World. The film begins with the organization of the operation and the stereotyped presentation of soldiers whose humanity is quickly painted and who are then caught up in the storm of urban warfare. Unlike in the book, the Somalis are mere shadows that shoot and, in return, get themselves killed, while every injured or killed American soldier is hyper-individualised. Nevertheless, by highlighting the solidarity between soldiers under fire, the cinematic portrayal depoliticises warfare. The question is then not to know why they are there nor what they are doing but how they are going to stay alive. War is no longer a 'continuation of politics by other means', but a 'natural' State, which is not subject to any questioning, where bravery, even the sanctity of American soldiers, and the cause they are fighting for, is laid bare.

*Black Hawk Down* is also a very effective and original film about ground combat because it belongs to a very rare number of American films on urban warfare. The capture of a town always poses the problem of the toughness of fighting and the losses it inflicts on the attackers.

Mogadishu is filmed by Ridley Scott as a trap closing around the soldiers, where the distinction between civilians and military is no longer relevant, and where the short distances between combatants increases dramatically the degree of violence of the fighting and civilian losses. It clearly involves informing public opinion about what urban operations in the Third World can be like, by emphasizing the intrinsic legitimacy of every American war but also the difficulty of keeping to the criteria of 'zero losses'.

On the other hand, all the final sequences of the film are dedicated to variations on the idea that the deaths of the soldiers, if they cannot be avoided, must not shake American determination to continue to wage war. Furthermore, the film ends by the departure of members of Delta Force for Mogadishu where they will start fighting afresh to find and liberate the American prisoners.

The other side of the process of rehabilitating war waged by Americans is found in Ridley Scott's vindication of the special forces. The film highlights this aspect of an American army that is no longer massive, but made up of young professionals whose expertise constitutes the United States military elite. The best among them appear as idealists who, by their actions, want to 'change things' and are there to help those who need it. The insistence on this type of discourse overshadows the real function of military forces, which are at the service of the State and must use armed force in an offensive or defensive manner, according to the orders received. If the existence of idealistic soldiers is not debatable, the army itself is not at the service of this idealism but of the State.

Special forces, in general, are hardly represented on screen, with the exception of marine reconnaissance forces, until the end of the 1990s. In fact, each armed service (Army, Navy, Air Force, Marines) has their own special forces. The perpetuation of competition, through the third party of film, happens by the advancement of these forces performances: *Black Hawk Down* establishes itself as an apology for elite Army troops as the only ones capable of leading future wars, which will take place in 'grey zones' of the planet. Furthermore, during an interview, Ridley Scott claims to have had the intention of preparing the public for this eventuality.

In doing this, he idealizes an appalling skirmish, with tragic consequences for the inhabitants of Mogadishu, and makes his own the attitude of filmmakers in the Reagan era of the 1980s, who imagined the ideal end to the Vietnam War by depicting urban warfare as a noble, martial universe, where the courage shown is such that it transcends defeat.

## American Strategy as Threat

Nevertheless, the rapid strategic reorientations imposed by the Bush administration on American strategy and its active, even militant, interventionism, created increasing anxiety in the midst of society, which expressed itself as much by uncritical enthusiasm as by open mistrust. This generalized ambivalence, mixed with the tendency for a certain distance between Washington and Hollywood, is seen in the production of films carrying several levels of meaning and whose real sense is not always the obvious one, while official discourse on the strategic threat and the 'axis of evil' becomes simpler.

This tendency is very noticeable in the second episode of George Lucas *Star Wars*, *Attack of the Clones* (2002), starring Ewan McGregor and Hayden Christensen. It is important to bear in mind that the scenario, the production and the filming were spread out between 1999 and 2001. The themes and the strategic ideas developed by the film already dominated the strategic debate. But their political actualization takes place at the same time as their cinematic one.

*Attack of the Clones* follows the trials of the Jedi knights, the guardians of the galactic republic, who find themselves unable to stem the tide of the increase in power of subversive forces led by Count Dooku and his mysterious master, who have gone across to the dark side of the Force and want to defeat the Republic by creating an alliance of planets. Obi wan Kenobi discovers that Count Dooku is in the process of creating a giant robot army on a distant desert-like planet to destroy the republican forces. The Jedi intervene and destroy the count's military-industrial organization with an army of clones that the former master of their order secretly financed. However, this mission only has the appearance of victory: at the same time, a young, very powerful Jedi apprentice, and in whom the threads of Destiny are gathered, is gradually going across to the dark side, whilst the president of the galactic Senate decides to employ the army of clones to fight against the breakaway planets. The Republic settles into war, the Jedi are divided, political officials are driven by duplicity, and the dark side of the Force infiltrates itself into hearts and minds, threatening everyone with the loss of the judgement required for the fight against evil.

Despite its often 'adolescent' appearance, *Attack of the Clones* combines the essential ingredients of the American strategic dilemma, namely the imperial temptation that weighs on military ultra-power when it is held by a progressively corrupt political body. The final sequence is a profoundly disturbing strategic commentary: the army of clones, led by Jedi officials, surrounds and destroys the desert planet, which is ruled by a hypocritical tyrant who is hiding the robotic weapons that are supposed to be used against the republic. The pseudo-republican army of clones win a crushing victory, thus increasing the power of politicians who are dedicated to a clandestine scheme to establish tyranny.

*Attack of the Clones* is a strategic and political fable that is aimed at the America of today. Real threat does not come from the outside, it is constructed by the highest levels of power who are tempted by tyranny. The army is presented as a body without conscience, which becomes the enemy of the republic when it is manipulated by a power which is no longer concerned about democratic control.

Interestingly, the war sequence in the desert, if it shows an easy military victory, is clearly shown as an essential step towards the overthrow of the republic, whilst the beaten enemy was only a political illusion, used to construct an artificial threat and thanks to which consensus is created in the heart of the galactic senate.

The other threat comes from the development of military technology through the impetus of biotechnologies, research in psychological conditioning and robotics. The army of clones is a metaphor for actual research and development activities into biological weapons, but also for constantly developing military training and conditioning, whilst the automated army echoes the actual perfecting of aerial, terrestrial and maritime drones, ultra-complex, automated weapons systems and robot defences which could, eventually, replace human soldiers. But this evolution towards an ever more penetrating technological dehumanization of the military poses questions about of its control by political powers and about its relation not only to American society, but also those in the countries where it will be used.

Finally, the military-imperial temptation is accentuated in the film in the way in which religiosity and spirituality is led astray. While the central power is shrouded in the cloak of dissimulation, secrecy and deception, it claims to look for the support of the Jedi, above all in the pursuit of wisdom, so as to apply it to the world of politics. But this lie makes political deviations those of spirituality, which is overlooked as a way of progressing towards enlightenment and instead becomes a means of learning madness and evil.

George Lucas' film in itself illustrates the move from the Reagan era to the presidency of George W Bush, even if the latter brought in to his administration many members of Reagan's and that of his father. While the rebel forces of the Republic destroyed the 'Evil Empire' in *Return of the Jedi* in 1983, in 2002 the absence of the 'Evil Empire' posed a fundamental political, strategic and ethical problem to the dominant power.

George Lucas makes his own the entire American philosophical tradition of mistrust and pessimism towards the State, particularly when the growth of its security and military component brings to bear the temptation of tyrannical deviations. He begins here the reprise of a cycle of films that are openly mistrustful of the national security system, at the time when the national security system is looking to renew its legitimacy so as to attack the 'axis of evil'.

## Pre-emptive Justice or the New Leviathan

We might have thought that the 11 September attacks would translate into overtly making heroes of the players in the national security game. Nothing of the sort happened. What is more, an important parallel strategic debate took hold around the failings of the secret services and the FBI, who were shown to have been incapable of arresting the terrorists, despite them having being on US soil for several months.

As a result, while the population was mainly supportive of the mission in Afghanistan, they also had doubts about those protecting them; but at the end of the war against the Taliban, the public was gradually brought round to the idea that reprisals had to be carried out against Saddam Hussein, and within months, 76 per cent of Americans ended up being persuaded of his collusion with Osama bin Laden in the preparation of the 11 September attacks. This development acted as the foundation for the presidential administration's preparations for the pre-emptive war against Iraq.

However, while President Bush and his ministers Colin Powell and Donald Rumsfeld (in the roles of 'good cop, bad cop') were mobilizing the army and the international community, opposition to the idea of attacking Iraq was being taken up with vigour by 40 per cent to 50 per cent of the public between September 2002 and February 2003, to the point where tens of thousands of people in New York, Washington and Los Angeles demonstrated against the preparations for war, a phenomenon not seen in the United States (except in Seattle in 1999) since the end of the demonstrations against the war in Vietnam.

These complex and contradictory currents also cut across areas of the national security system. The doctrine of pre-emptive war is based on the idea that a certain number of States present an unacceptable threat for the United States because they are hostile and possess weapons of mass destruction (as is the case in the US and most industrialized countries, whether they are allied to America or not), whose existence is known about by the American secret services. And it is here that the shoe pinches for many national security officials.

In this way, the CIA had been looking for years at reports that highlighted the large disarmament of Iraqi defence forces. Weapons of mass destruction were dismantled after being effectively located by the UN. But this accumulation of proof was regularly disqualified because of the 'intimate convictions' of political officials. This was reinforced after Donald Rumsfeld set up an information-gathering service similar to the intelligence at the Pentagon, which accumulated precisely the material that the CIA and the Defense Intelligence Agency judged to be unreliable, even unfounded. But the political advantage of this material was that it allowed the open assertion of the existence of real threats where traditional institutions saw nothing at all.

These tensions between hawks and moderates, interventionists and the anti-war faction put Hollywood in a delicate situation at the time when the studios were discreetly adopting greater independence from political power, while wishing to ensure the good favour of the public – all without incurring reprisals.

These tensions imbue Doug Liman's *The Bourne Identity*, 2002, starring Matt Damon. An adaptation of the best-seller by Robert Ludlum, the great spy novelist and enthusiastic denigrator of the national security system, it is about a young man, Jason Bourne, who is picked up in the Mediterranean by a crew of fishermen. He is suffering from amnesia, without name nor memory, but is infinitely gifted in the art of survival and combat. He gradually learns that he is a former killer for an undercover operations branch of the CIA. His last mission led him to France to execute an African head of State who was threatening to make sensational revelations if the CIA did not put him back in power. Jason Bourne, hunted down by other super-killers like him, manages to escape and kill the head of the 'undercover' department, Treadstone, whose existence is instantly forgotten, glossed over and denied by the CIA, which goes on seamlessly to other projects.

In contrast to films of the 1970s like *The Deer Hunter*, *The Bourne Identity* does not present the CIA as isolated from the rest of the security system, but divided while it leads its own secret war in Africa. Curiously, this war pits CIA agents directly against Africans. Although the film unfolds almost entirely in Paris, the French are absent from the confrontation. This secret war appears completely illegitimate and subject to the risks of the contradictions of US foreign policy towards Africa. Above all, it is led by personnel who do not officially exist and are subject to specific, mainly dehumanizing, conditioning. Furthermore, Jason Bourne lost his memory following his inability to carry out another State-sanctioned murder, and the quest to regain his memory is also a quest for his lost humanity. Similarly, the CIA is grey, cold and bureaucratic; its only purpose seems to be to achieve objectives which are not subject to any real counter-balance.

Consequently, a denunciation unfurls just beneath the surface of the security system that, undoubtedly, lost its *raison d'être* long ago and became a parallel State, a master of its varied and contradictory foreign policies, conducting useless experiments of dehumanization on young Americans to further its subversive activities of abroad and on US soil.

This development is evoked several times when the budgets required for undercover operations and the training of secret killers are recalled. The budgets are, on the evidence, clandestine; they are thus not controlled by Congress, which decides the funding given to US defence and security institutions through commissions which are very vigilant most of the time and jealously guard their authority. The problem raised is thus that of the confidence that American system, and also its allies, like France, can accord to institutions which have a non-democratic concept of politics.

In addition, the director highlights the dimension of double discourse and the systematic recourse to lying by the CIA, as much in its departments as in justifying its actions to the outside world. This way of disappearing into obscurity is shown in the figure of Jason Bourne, who is constantly looking for the truth, which has been hidden by the superimposed methods of the production of lies that makes the State a theatre of shadow puppets. It is also undoubtedly not by chance if all the lies are exposed not in Washington but in Paris, the City of Light.

This problem of the world of defence, security and intelligence being viewed as a 'empire of lies' coincides in synchronic fashion with the deployment of anti-Iraqi rhetoric from Washington in autumn 2002 and the constantly-repeated justifications of pre-emptive war.

This fundamental problem of lies and politics in a democratic regime tormented by the temptation of imperialism is at the centre of Steven Spielberg's *Minority Report* (2001), an adaptation of the book by Philip K. Dick, the science fiction author who, in all his works, explores the effects of subverting reality by the collective spread of fantasies. Steven Spielberg makes the film the odyssey, in the not too distant future, of a policeman who heads a city police unit in Washington. This unit, due to 'precogs', mutant psychics capable of seeing murders which have not happened yet with great accuracy, is brought in to arrest potential killers and jail them before they can commit their crimes. It makes the police and the justice system seen pre-emptive.

The system is supposed to be foolproof because it is impossible to forge. In fact, it is tainted from the beginning, since its creator, a powerful criminologist, must have killed the mother of one of the 'precogs' in order to take possession of the child and set up the operation whose extension he recommends to the whole of the federal judicial system. He is eventually denounced by the head of the pre-emptive unit, who he tried to trap so as to keep his crime a secret. When the truth comes out, the criminologist kills himself, and the 'pre-emptive prisoners' are freed, because the crimes, of which they are accused before they have been committed, cannot be proved nor shown after the fact.

*Minority Report* sets out its intrigue at an historic junction. While preventive policing is still only an experiment limited to the district of Washington, it is on the point of becoming a unique coercive force possessing the 'monopoly of legitimate violence', capable of anticipating all violence other that its own and keeping that violence in an unrealized State, while leading the peaceful organization of reality through law and order. To do this, the guilty are pinpointed, and history becomes the subject of over-determination of the State, which is depicted as a sort of benevolent Big Brother.

But, in concrete terms, the masters of preventive designation become masters of violence: they arbitrarily manipulate consciousnesses, ethical standards and public opinion, all the while proclaiming the inherent wisdom of crime prevention. They have recourse to practices based on the arbitrary designation of successive scapegoats, and from which no individual can protect himself, given that he cannot provide proof that he is not about to commit the crime that has not yet taken place.

Steven Spielberg's film puts itself as much in the American history of anti-tyrannical political commentary as in the most immediate current affairs of autumn 2002 and the amassing of American troops around Iraq. It demonstrates the manipulative tautology on which the idea of 'pre-emptive State coercion' rests, which can only be democratically justified by a wide-scale intoxication of public opinion, built around uninterrupted media hype. In this way, Spielberg's Washington is covered with advertising hoardings which proclaim the necessity for and the legitimacy of the 'precogs'.

However, while the film is a charge against State certainties justifying preventive violent actions, while the American army machine prepares its vast encirclement of Iraq itself throughout the entire Persian Gulf, Steven Spielberg declares himself in favour of pre-emptive military action. His sincerity is not the issue: as an eminent American, head of the very powerful Dreamworks studio, and as a simple American citizen, filled with the conformism that is part of this society, he is looking above all to give himself, and thus his business, a consensual appearance.

This step is particularly important at a time when Washington was ruled by a militant Republican party, which, in the collective memory of Hollywood, was associated with the dark years of McCarthyism and with purges of whole studios. The concept of pre-emptive coercion is unavoidably called into question by Steven Spielberg's film, despite his official declarations in favour of the doctrine of pre-emptive war, which reflects the trend that has already been taking place for a number of years: prudent, discreet but important distancing between the powers of cinema and politics.

At the same time, an association of actors and directors led by Sean Penn, the famous actor and courageous but isolated anti-establishment figure, was set up in order to denounce the 'lies of the Bush administration'. Sean Penn himself went to Iraq and made more pronouncements against any intervention in the country. He was followed by actors, scriptwriters and directors, some of whom set up a travelling theatre troupe which performed Aristophanes' *Lysistrata*, a satirical play in which the women of Athens decide to 'prevent' future wars by going on sex strike against their husbands. But these attitudes were very much in the minority and did not create a real movement; the confrontation frightened the studios, who feared reprisals that would call back into question their strategy of discreet distancing.

This mistrust towards the American Leviathan, this State which is able to be formidably coercive as much against its own citizens as against certain members of the international community, was stirred up by the way in which the Bush administration incorporated North Korea into the 'axis of evil'. This small State, the last Socialist regime on earth inspired by Stalin, also managed to become a nuclear and ballistic power. It was now equipped with missiles capable of reaching Japan, and appeared to possess several nuclear weapons. It was impossible to know their effectiveness as they had never been tested. Nevertheless, their existence transformed North Korea into a *de facto* member of the club of those States possessing nuclear weapons of mass destruction.

North Korea managed in this way to embody the very substance of the prevailing definition of threat in the American strategic debate: it had technological, industrial and military capabilities whose development escaped American control. It had managed to establish itself at the same time as a threat, both in nuclear and capacity terms, and as such, it obtained the mesured treatment that every nuclear power accords to other nuclear powers.

The national security system's fear of North Korea is encapsulated to good effect by James Bond in Lee Tamahori's *Die Another Day* (2002), starring Pierce Brosnan and Halle Berry. The British secret agent is sent to North Korea to assassinate a young colonel who is building a stockpile of the latest weapons in order to launch an offensive against South Korea, whose border is protected by American forces under the command of the UN. As a result of treachery, for the first time in his life, 007 is arrested and tortured for months on end. He escapes and tracks down the Korean colonel, who has begun an extraordinary operation to acquire for the North Korean army a satellite equipped with an ultra-powerful laser canon, which is capable of destroying both missiles launched against it and ground forces. James Bond kills him (in horrifying fashion; he was asking for it!) just as he is launching the offensive against the border.

This film demonstrates furthermore that, if North Korean weapons have reached these peaks of technological effectiveness, it is through the coopera tion of western high-tech weapons and money-laundering industries. James Bond is in fact charged with regulating the perverse effects of western transnationalized interests when they meet the strategic projects of Third World countries bent on revenge; the external threat appears to be clearly sustained by the American system, or in wider terms, the 'western' one.

But those in charge of the American national security system preferred to ignore this aspect of the film. On December 18 2002, that is to say about one month after the film hit the screens, the Defense Secretary, Donald Rumsfeld, declared that Americans had nothing to worry about because 'North Korean missiles cannot reach American soil beyond Alaska'. This declaration was curious at this time, insofar as North Korea had not demonstrated any particular desire to attack the United States with nuclear weapons. It was explained with reference to the film that presents North Korean aggression as highly dangerous, and Donald Rumsfeld used the fear it aroused in order to prepare the public for another event.

In effect, this declaration was given its full sense two days later when President Bush signed the order to deploy the first four anti-missile missile bases that were supposed to be the foundation for NMD, the tests for which had never yet been conclusive. At the same time, by stressing the adoption of a defensive military position towards North Korea, the Defense Secretary deviated from the doctrine of pre-emptive war in order to set himself up in the traditional logic of nuclear deterrent and negotiations.

In this way, at a time when American foreign policy was fraught with major tensions, the cinema industry played a part in the construction of consensus to a certain extent, but had a serious tendency to see threat more in the projects of State than those from outside the US. This poses the fundamental question of how Hollywood views the State.

# 9

# THE STATE AND DEFENCE: QUESTIONS OF LEGITIMACY

The American State is simultaneously the product of the American Revolution of 1776, the conquest of the West, the massacre of American-Indians and wars against the British then the Mexican empire. It established itself by crushing the Confederation during the American Civil War and in pursuing its triumphal advance beyond the Pacific with the war against the Spanish in the Philippines and Cuba.

If, as Geoffrey Peret writes, the United States is 'a country made by war',[1] it would be even more correct to attribute this expression to the State. The American State's relationship with war is thus consubstantial, but profoundly unique, because it has hardly had to defend itself from outside enemies. From the end of the nineteenth century, the culture of war was strictly of an expeditionary Nature, which examines the definition of defence and thus the justification of the State's military power. In addition, the State being seen as carrying the seeds of tyranny, its Nature, in Max Weber's view, as the 'monopoly of legitimate violence', which is taken for granted in Europe and Asia, is a lot less so in the United States, where the State causes fear.

But by assuming the tasks of security and defence which justifies the existence of an army, the federal State asserts itself as the protector of American society. This concept being developed from the beginnings of American history through its sense of being elected by God, the State is presented a complex character, both profane and sacred, necessary and terrifying, a potential tyrant and bulwark of democracy.

For about 50 years, national security cinema has shown the different contradictory aspects of the State and become a continuous, effective commentary on the State's dilemma. The State, which has existed for barely two centuries, has to guarantee its basic defensive function while being confronted by the very ideals of American civilization (including a strong resistance to the idea of the State's vocation to lead, even control, society) and by endeavouring to establish its grip on the rest of the world. These tensions are the subject of a permanent working on screen that plays a part in the life of the State and the debate about its legitimacy.

## The National Security State, from Reality to Image

The profound originality of American national security cinema resides in its creation of a highly dramatic portrayal of the life of defence and security institutions, even the most secret of them. In addition, these productions articulate this rational approach to unbridled dramatic and heroic make-believe with perfect sociological and political precision. National security cinema films the CIA, the Pentagon, the presidency, special forces units and the various armed services, but also the Senate commissions on armed forces or the activities of the intelligence community, and sometimes the military-industrial organization.

Through cinema, the production of the American State's strategic culture becomes a public spectacle that is addressed to a nationwide audience, expressed by private enterprises which transnatiozalize it. While, by definition, the national security universe, thus State coercion, secures a certain opacity for itself, it paradoxically finds itself constantly in the spotlight, in which it actively participates.

National security cinema has made these institutions the main protagonists in a long-running production about the life of the State, in the fundamental aspect that is, following Max Weber again, the legitimate monopolization of violence, in order to ensure the continuation of the social *status quo*. But, in the same way, security and defence activities maintain a secret, concealed and mysterious air. Films showing the main security agencies are particularly revealing. Since the 1980s, the CIA and the National Security Agency (NSA) have become the generic subjects for this type of cinema, where they are similarly in competition.

The CIA has a very particular political, strategic and cinematic status which imbues all of its component parts, and who are elevated to the level of heroes that Hollywood demands. The best example of this is the character of Jack Ryan, created by Tom Clancy at the end of the 1980s. Successive adaptations of his books – *The Hunt for Red October, Clear and Present Danger, The Sum of All Fears* – constitute a giant, both literary and cinematic, work, and complement each other by creating an 'imaginary' CIA, which is the counterpoint to the actual history of the Agency at this time.

From the end of the 1980s and the Gulf War, the CIA thus becomes the media and political world's favourite target, simultaneously reproaching it for its inability to predict the collapse of the Soviet Union, the fall of the Berlin Wall and the invasion of Kuwait, the incompetence of its agents or its most implausible moles (like Aldrich Ames, an alcoholic who helped himself to armfuls of files in order to sell them on to the Russians. He led an indiscreet lifestyle and continued working for years before being arrested). Conversely, the films and books of the 'Jack Ryan' series, while affecting a certain realism, stress the Agency's importance in the protection of the United States.

This intention, as much from the author as from the filmmakers who adapt his works, responds to the need to make the CIA a 'normal' State bureaucracy whose agents are citizens like any other and not the black heart of a terrifying national and international conspiracy. Author and director alike thus work on the 'de-demonization' of the CIA, taking it out of the shadowy legend of it created throughout the Cold War, where it actually contributed to the transnationalization of the secret war against the USSR in Europe, Africa and Asia, while bringing to their knees Latin American regimes who were not sufficiently pro-American. These activities, carried out at the behest of those in power, but without structural political control, made the CIA of the time a tyrannical State within a State.

The CIA needed to extricate itself from this role and image when the secret war had ended because of the fall of the USSR, although the studios tried to carry on the excellent dramatic and legitimate potential it encapsulated, as much as the bulwark of the nation as tyrannical risk. The CIA of the Reagan years completed a sort of 'voyage to the end of the night' by its illegal support for the Nicaraguan Contras, the extreme right wing junta of El Salvador and the regime of Manuel Noriega in Panama, encouraging drug trafficking to finance them. It helped the Islamist mujahadeen in Afghanistan, was linked to Pakistani and Chinese extremists, and developed collaborations with the worst regimes of South-East Asia, including Burma and Indonesia. This transnationalization of the worst aspects of American State power between the 1950s and the end of the 1980s was justified, and often experienced sincerely by those effecting it, as a response to the threat of geopolitical encirclement of the US on the global stage to which the USSR was suspected of systematic involvement.

The Jack Ryan books ensure then a change in the future of the CIA in a filmed and idealized history which gets it off the hook of so many years of scandal. In this way, *The Hunt for Red October* hit the bookstands in 1987, at the time when the CIA's reputation was tarnished by the Irangate scandal. Its adaptation by John McTiernan in 1990 established the shadowy world of secrecy on the right side of State life.

This project was made possible by work on framing and lighting. The CIA is filmed as a labyrinth of dimly-lit corridors but also of discreet, welcoming offices where highly professional, basically benevolent workers predominate. The film's originality is thus, among other things, its description of daily activities. CIA officials and agents are shown as tough people, conscious of the need to think in terms of power and strategy relations, slightly cynical, but not excessively so, and who never abandon certain broadly humanist principles. The Agency sees itself given respectability and a reassuring normality, which anchors the world of the secret to that of American daily life.

This process is underscored by the follow-up, *Patriot Games* (1992), where Jack Ryan's family is at the heart of the intrigue and where the description of his daily professional life is developed throughout the film. But Philip Noyce films the CIA very differently from John McTiernan. We emerge from the subterranean; CIA life takes place in large, well-lit offices, in vast, bright spaces divided into cubicles that make informal meetings and brainstorming sessions easier, and those in charge pay attention to the elegance of their efficient secretaries. Meeting rooms still exist from where undercover operations are followed by satellites, but they are only rarely frequented, and with a noticeable reticence, by people who know the value of human life.

This warm, professional life is extended into the private sphere; Jack Ryan is a fine head of household, his wife is an eye surgeon, their children are charming and they are seen doing their homework. The rooms of their house are high-ceilinged, light and tastefully furnished. There is an accurate description in this of the family environment of the upper-middle-class WASP, whose fortunes are regularly improved by comings and goings between the public and private sector. The brightness of the spaces ensures the continuity between work and family, which helps to transform the secret work of intelligence into any other type of office work.

When the Irish extremists attack his family, Jack Ryan reacts as head of household, State agent and coercion specialist, these three aspects merging into one and erasing the singular appearance of an individual reaction which is effectively that of the State, in its most coercive and legitimate form. The use of armed violence thus acquires an obvious and ethically simplistic character, associating the will of the father to protect his family to the will of the CIA, that is the State, to help him, because the film presents the Agency as existing solely for that purpose.

This portrait of the 'good State' is qualified with *Clear and Present Danger* (1994). The interior architecture of the Agency becomes a maze again, offices are locked: it is the time of in-fighting, secret, illegal operations and power struggles.

In addition, the interior spaces of the State filmed here are no longer only those of the CIA, but also of the White House, which is itself a modern day Daedalus. Personnel close to the highest levels of power are no longer shown in the light of reassuring normality: they are totally identified by their functions and the interests which result from them. Daily life at the executive level no longer has anything to do with that of the bureaucracy of security and defence; it is about a twilight world of semi-darkness. It is only in the radiant warmth of the family home that life has its place again.

*Clear and Present Danger*, by the way in which it films bureaucratic and political life, explores the other side of the national security State, that is the 'bad State', where power circumvents or tries to evade the law. The law is shown in the form of the head of the Senate Commission on intelligence activities who, from her elevated rostrum, accepts Jack Ryan's revelations under oath and, using her authority, moderates the presidential proneness to autocracy and that of the CIA for illegal clandestine activities. The law is the standard that ultimately regulates national security activities, by defining what is allowed and what is forbidden, good and evil, democratic and tyrannical, and which sets the price for any transgression.

The relationship with the law is represented by cinema as the pivot between the 'good' State and the 'bad' State. *JFK*, by Oliver Stone (1991), is entirely constructed around the duel between the national security system and the State of law and justice, and seeks to show that the assassination of John F. Kennedy was sought and prepared by the national security system, and supported by Johnson, who, once president, allegedly 'granted' the Vietnam War to the military and the military-industrial organization. The film follows Judge Garrison, depicted as a virtuous lover of the law, fighting against the lies of State that allow all the aberrations of a power tempted by autonomy and tyranny. The voice of Judge Garrison becomes that of the law and justice, which re-establishes order inside the State, in the name of a superior ideal of justice and virtue.

The filming emphasizes the radical dichotomy existing between those who have taken on board this standard and those who try to evade it. The distinction between two normative tendencies, legalist or tyrannical, is the matrix of practices which makes the national security State that of the 'City upon a Hill', or of a possible tyranny when it is subjected to unusual tensions.

## Destruction and Resilience of the State

Through its scripts, national security cinema establishes itself as a continuous and virtual examination of the State. The State operates by inventing risks and mortal enemies who are as much imaginations of the endangerment or destruction of both society and the State. A large part of security cinema rests on the face-to-face encounter between the State and destructive danger.

An excellent example of this is Mimi Leder's *Deep Impact* (1998), starring Morgan Freeman and Tea Leoni, filmed at the same time as *Armageddon*, the year when Space Command was itself given the responsibility of watching out for celestial bodies that could crash into Earth.

A giant asteroid is going to smash into Earth and annihilate the human race; there are two years left to destroy it. At the same time, the State prepares for its survival by creating a network of subterranean bases. The drama is followed from the perspective of a female journalist who details the increasing panic of civilian society and the mobilization of the State which is looking to control these divisions while preparing the survival of the political, strategic, university and specialist elite. A space expedition finally manages to pulverize the asteroid, a large fragment of which sinks into the Atlantic, triggering off a gigantic tidal wave which submerges Washington. However, it is the least damage caused.

The last sequence of the film is a presidential address which, in a benevolent tone, salutes the ability of the American people to recover from hardship and reconstruct. The allusions to the catastrophe interpreted as a new Flood are numerous and make a new Biblical patriarch of the president. The direct descendants of the Biblical prophets and that of the founding fathers are found in him; as head of State, he crafts the re-foundation of the United States, the nation of 'Manifest Destiny'.

The film transcends the concept of State in the modern sense of an institutional apparatus in charge of the protection and reproduction of society acquiring its resources from taxation and gives it a sacred dimension. Through the person of the president, the American State asserts itself as the vehicle and guarantor of America's status as an elected nation. The presidential Word becomes both a spiritual and political statement, which heralds the arrival of a new age after the purification by ordeal not only of the United States but especially of Washington, whose ruins and reconstruction work provide the backdrop for this last sequence.

The renewal of the link between the United States and God is expressed in pragmatic terms in this work (Americans talk about *practicality*). The State apparatus methods and work strives for the accomplishment of American Destiny. This pragmatic and Protestant concept of divine intent being spread in the world by human travails, is epitomized in the image of cranes and scaffolding which are reconstructing Capitol Hill, the seat of Congress, in other words the representatives of this new elect.

At the same time, in order to undertake and successfully overcome these ordeals, by renewing the link between the US and God, the State can only use national security to constitute the arsenal and human means through which destruction will be averted.

In a wider sense, the State's ability to confront destruction and to 'weave its resilience' around the personality of the president, that is to take up the course of its existence again by atoning for itself in and despite the ordeal and eventually using the ordeal itself as the basis for its resilience, is the subject of regular contemplation by Hollywood, which, objectively, is a support for the power of the State over American society.

## Strategy, Politics and Religion: The Hegemony of National Security

By becoming a national security State from the end of the Second World War (and precisely in 1947, with the vote for the National Security Act), the US federal State effectively began to conceive of and spread a political and strategic ideology of threat: it created a corpus of discourse and official military and political representations allowing the clear identification of the threat and the enemy. The State thus produced the standards of threat.

These standards are taken up by the cinema industry as dramatic material. What is more, American cinema being always remarkably precise sociologically, it takes account of the most significant phenomena but also the most subtle at work in the depths of a collective American mentality, dominated by a feeling of omnipresent threat. Cinema subjects the culture of threat to a standardizing process, to enable for the spectacle to be understood and accepted by the majority of the public.

This heavy-handed approach is articulated politically and cinematically by the federal State in the form of discourses and practices, and by Hollywood which confers on them a particular significance because of the power of images and catharsis. The images produced by the studios in the form of collective spectacles are both standardized by the political and normative ISN'T SOMETHING LACKING? They give an obvious character to the ideology of security.

*The Peacemaker* (1997) by Mimi Leder, with George Clooney and Nicole Kidman, is a good example of cinematic prescriptivism. A Defence Intelligence Agency agent and a nuclear strategy specialist are tracking a group of terrorists in Eastern Europe, Russia, central Asia, then on the streets of Manhattan. The terrorists are working with the Russia mafia and mercenaries who have stolen a Russian nuclear weapon. During their trip, they discover the existence of a whole series of interlinking criminal networks, who specialize in the transfer of the latest technology and are prepared to serve any paymaster. The people behind the network are in fact ex-Yugoslavs who want to blow up the UN headquarters in New York in order to avenge their abandonment to Serbian forces during the war in Bosnia.

The film was produced at the time when the creation of strategic discourses was dominated by the idea that instability, networks and terrorists constituted the current standard of the new strategic threat, since they can cut across and inundate American society with strategies of subversion and methods of 'undetectable' destruction. American society also depends on instability and networks of all sorts of things, whether they are material, electronic or of information. This instability is then considered as carrying threats in so far as it is possible to predict that this interdependence will backfire on the United States. The very existence of these instabilities ensures the transition from the local to the global, from potential to real terror, from resources to the threat.

This post-modern concept of threat is, *de facto*, fairly abstract, since clandestine instabilities, by definition, cannot be seen. Cinema replaces this semi-invisibility by stories and dramatic images, and at the same time highlights the norm by maintaining a discourse which, at least at first sight, is stereotypical.

It shows the general public these threats as well as the positive actions of the State. These images and their political and strategic content, become a common reference point, an essential element of a mass, industrial and political culture. Through cinema, the national security State is established as an essential collective figure in the mental universe of Americans. In its security role, it takes on a mythological importance by acting as the continuation and renewal of the story of the origins of the State. *The Peacemaker* is the messenger of this myth, which has been reworked and standardised by awareness of the globalisation of instability and criminalisation, to which the trans-nationalisation of the American security apparatus responds. The story of its extension to central Asia, through American bases in Turkey and their helicopters which the US agents use to get into the continent, is related like a system of material and ideological circumstances for the benefit of people's salvation, from American civilian society and the international community through the rescue of the UN. At the same time, the salvation is spiritual: the sequence when the nuclear bomb is defused takes place inside a Manhattan church. It assures the continuity between strategy, security and spirituality: the national security agents, in securing the bomb, become members of a strange clergy, where security practices act as the liturgy. Furthermore, the defusing of the bomb follows stereotypes which codify all scenes of this type, like in *Abyss*, *Armageddon* and others, acting equally as suspense and ritual.

There is here a revival of the myth of the American strategic system as the global means for the salvation of mankind. Max Weber defines the Church as the 'legitimate monopoly of the manipulation of the goods of salvation', but this salvation of mankind, in America's case, comes from the strict responsibility of the religious sphere; cinema extends it to the sphere of national security through stories with mythological content. The national security State is evoked as a medium working for the salvation of the City upon a Hill, because it has the legitimate monopoly of 'manipulation of the military and security means of salvation'.

This constant to-ing and fro-ing from the strategic to the spiritual is always put to the fore by apologist film-makers like Roland Emmerich. In *Independence Day*, the lengthy final battle sequence between the Air Force and the extraterrestrials, upon which the fate of the world as much as that of the United States depends, is preceded by a speech by the president to the forces he will lead into combat. During the speech, there is a makeshift prayer circle inside the base which includes an old Jewish man who re-discovers his faith and begins to speak to God again, children and the very Waspish head of the CIA. At the same time, a pilot and his partner receive the sacrament of marriage in the presence of a couple of married friends, who rediscover at that moment the meaning of their own union. The husband is furthermore the Jewish computer expert who perfected the asymmetric strategy which will annihilate the defences of the adversary; his computer virus is a new version of the spirit of revolt of David and the trumpets which knocked down the walls of Jericho. The preparation for combat finds itself in this way to be the moment of renewal of the processes of association which founded the first groups in society and their sacrament. By preparing themselves to destroy the extraterrestrials, American society, seen in its nomadic and military roots, renews its alliance with God.

The national security machine's preparation for survival and combat is thus as much a process for the salvation of the citizen's lives as a sacrament and intimate movement of heroes towards transcendence. Even in a film apparently as 'secular' as *The Sum of All Fears*, the treatment of the image at once brings about the relationship of the State to a mystery on which the salvation of everyone depends. The Kremlin is photographed like a church, immense and sombre. The occupants, but also the American visitors are all dressed in black, as Orthodox monks would be. The seat of the Russian high command is an almost entirely black crypt, where the crisis is experienced like a 'lesson of darkness'. On the other hand, the emergency operations room of the White House, and by extension the meeting room of Air Force One, is a considerably smaller, confined space, principally devoted solely to strategic decision-making. The president however seeks to be alone to pray in order to be sure of making the right decisions. Air Force One becomes here a space of war and prayer where the means of the 'monopoly of legitimate violence' are concentrated, which becomes those of the 'goods of salvation'.

This Hollywood concept of the sacred Nature of the State, which fits in to post-modern political thought, is at the heart of the very strange *Reign of Fire* (2001) by Rob Bowman, with Christian Bale and Matthew MacConaghey. Bowman directed the cult 'X-Files' television series, which explored all the illuminating and murky facets of the national security State, by distinguishing between 'good' and 'evil' conspiracies.

At the beginning of the twenty first century, a buried dragon is unearthed during work on the London Underground. A few months later, hundreds of thousands of dragons, who feed on ashes, burst forth from the earth and lay the world to waste. Fifteen years later, humanity is dying out, when a young, passionate Englishman gathers together a small community who try to survive by subsisting in a country house north of London. One day, an armoured column of the American national guard suddenly appears, led by a knowledgeable commander, who has brought his team in a C-130 air transporter from Minnesota to England, despite the dragons dominating the skies. These Americans have discovered the dragon's Achilles heel: they are all female, with the exception of one male who impregnates them and assures the biological survival of the species. This dragon is in London where the armoured column is heading before it is obliterated in a jet of flames and the dragon turns against the small community of Britons. The British and American survivors then share their weapons and march on the capital. The fight with the grand dragon begins. The surviving American sacrifices himself and the Beast is beaten by the young Englishman, the 'prince' of his community. The film ends on the resumption of communications between the British and French communities.

This film thus makes reference to the founding mythology of the national security State and to political and historical genealogy. The dragons are the essence of threat: they are the symbol of dangerous Nature, whose anger can sweep away vulnerable and flimsy human society, but they are also the 'demons of the earth' that Saint George and Saint Michael had to slay. The emergence of a warrior caste which is at the same time in charge of the political thus finds itself given legitimacy.

In addition, the film highlights the British origins of the mindset of the State of war. Americans are the nomadic soldiers of the national guard, the militia of the Revolution of 1776, and they make an alliance with the British 'city-state'. The American strategy is put in check by the dragons; it is the strategy of descendants of those whose founding fathers wanted to liberate themselves which leads to victory, survival and nobility, that is, to a superior status. A new form of Christianity develops within the British community-State: every evening, communal prayer takes place in order to repeat the imperative that is the necessity to watch and to adapt to the sky. In order to recover from the terrible shock of the massive attack, the survivors pray together before leaving to fight. We witness here an interpretation of the origins of the State, which are also, from an American cinema perspective, the origins of religion, spirituality and war.

It follows that, through cinema, national security sees itself given as much a strategic vocation as a theological and spiritual one. National security portrayed by cinema appears as one of the forms of American religiosity, an instrument through which the American will for accomplishment is expressed and the divine will to see the US triumph in the tests that it is sent. In this, national security is interpreted as if it was a Church, without any clearly-designated clergy. The State, national security and religion finally end up being considered as one and the same by this type of cinema.

National security cinema is revealed to be a way of magnifying and sublimating the defence and security system. The Pentagon and the CIA are in themselves bureaucracies of State, and not only have little, or no, means of establishing a real transcendental character – compared with the president, who pledges his oath on the Bible before Congress, swearing to respect the Constitution. The cinema picks up on this by giving them an image which makes them break free from their strictly monopolistic, terrestrial status of means of coercion and indiscretion.

It is at this very deep intricate level of grand strategy, religion and cinema where the interdependence between Hollywood and national security is played out.

By giving itself this role, the cinema industry assumes a religious function in the literal sense of the Latin term *religere*: it 'joins together' tens of millions of cinema-goers or those who watch or rewatch the films on television and on video, by showing strategic threats and portraying the State as a benevolent or dangerous power, images which all at the same time are standardized and prescriptive, and constantly produced, distributed and sold at the national and international level. Because of this industry, the American people can commune in the spectacle of national security and in this way live together as a nation.

In the last 50 years, this type of cinema has become one of the essential vehicles for the political dominance of national security by defending as much its political as its ethical and religious character and by creating a spectacle whose standards are accepted by everyone. These norms are the heroization of the agents of State, their sacred character if they do not deviate from the strict defence of American citizens, the on-screen portrayal of threat, as it is officially defined and sustained by the American collective imagination.

At the same time, this sublimation establishes national security and the image of the State in a situation of dependence towards to Hollywood. To a certain extent, Washington consents to subjugating itself to the hegemony of the cinema industry.

This turnaround in power relations has happened between the McCarthy era, which showed the State to be domineering, and the most recent period, where the studios tried for a certain prudent autonomy, acquired by creating a universe of images where the American State is an invincible, mythological force. Here resides the unique Nature of American power where politics, strategy, the image industry and the imaginary intertwine.

# 10

# EMPIRE, WAR AND REVOLUTION

The American attack and occupation of Iraq is concomitant with complex internal political developments, which bring into play the most conflicting tendencies and the most radical American political traditions and models. While the American strategic system has been working since the end of the Vietnam War to free itself from involvement with the places onto which it projects its military power, the occupation of Iraq has led to a deep crisis, which is seen in the revival of the question of the legitimacy of US political power at the beginning of the twenty-first century. At the same time, reactions to the policies of the Bush government are revitalizing the deepest layer of American political culture: the question of revolution.

This questioning is at the heart of Antoine Fuqua's complex work, *Tears of the Sun* (2003), starring Bruce Willis and Monica Belluci. The film follows the trials of the captain of a small, elite Navy unit, who is ordered to rescue an Italian doctor with American citizenship from a forest village during a civil war in Nigeria. Refusing to abandon her patients and be taken to safety by helicopter, the doctor persuades the group captain to lead her and the refugees through the forest as far as the border with Cameroon. However, they are followed by a platoon of genocidal Nigerian soldiers, who want to execute the heir of a very powerful clan, who is among the column of refugees.

The march through the jungle, war and the beginning of a rural genocide sets in motion a radical political process among the captain and his men. In effect, instead of following the orders of their chain of command, the soldiers close ranks around their leader, and, while the enemy approaches and the trap is about to close around them, the captain starts a political debate on why they are there and what they are doing. He refuses to abandon the refugees even if that involves going against direct orders. Instead, he decides to escort them to the border in an attempt to ensure their survival. The military unit is transformed by this process into a micro warrior democracy, an 'African-Athens' in miniature, and the former American soldiers become bound up with the communal Destiny of this small group of Africans. One black soldier declares: 'They are my people, I refuse to leave them!' Tracked at close quarters, the soldiers and the refugees will eventually be saved by the air strikes the captain has requested, and which are granted, in spite of his insubordination, by the naval group commander posted off the Nigerian coast.

This sequence of dramas conveys the film's very dense political content. The soldier mutiny in the name of solidarity with the Africans replays the American revolution, but also the foundation of American society, which is inextricably linked to the development of slavery. Faced with the reality of civil war, the American soldiers lose the insensitiveness that they have acquired through combat. The primary group they form ceases to be shut off from the outside world but opens up to the human reality surrounding it. While they were subject to an unremitting process of brutalization, the horror of civil war and genocide affects them through their sudden awareness of a shared humanity with the people they are escorting. The political and strategic consequence which results from it is their decision to fight, even to die, for them. In so doing, the Nigerian jungle becomes the place where 'homo americanus' is re-established, by becoming the Frontier where American history can be replayed, this time by avoiding slavery and genocide, the two 'sins of foundation'. This is particularly evident during a sequence where the soldiers intervene against a band of murderers who burn, rape and cut the throats of villagers belonging to a persecuted ethnic group.

In this way, what is enisaged is the re-establishment of the American Republic according to real principles of equality and justice, in an effect to avoid the brutality of constructing a nation dominated by whites and numerous forms of coercion. The projection of force thus becomes the vehicle for an internal political enterprise, where the nation's redevelopment is indissociable from an individual's contemplation on the significance of his actions and life. It is noteworthy that the Navy is presented as the vehicle for this revival of American revolutionary culture, being *de facto* the most democratic armed force there is, insofar as it cannot act on the territorial aspect of American State power. The maritime bulwark of the republic and democracy also becomes its crucible. At the end of the film, once they have crossed the border between Nigeria and Cameroon, the refugees are left in the capable hands of the French Foreign Legion, whilst the last shot shows the Bruce Willis character stretched out on the floor of a helicopter, held maternally in the arms of the modern Pieta, Monica Belluci, the agony of this both internal journey and actual combat operation having left its mark. There is nothing surprising here: the film-maker thus creates the appearance of the sacred dimension inherent in the revolutionaries who reinvest the American nation with its mythical significance.

The story of this projection of ideal force takes place in the context of the invasion and occupation of Iraq. The Bush administration has repeatedly sought to justify and legitimize its stance towards Iraq: Saddam Hussein is alleged to have accumulated an arsenal of weapons of mass destruction and prepared an attack against the United States; Iraq is alleged to be the geo-political key that would allow democracy to be spread and established by the United States in the whole of the Middle East, thus assimilating the standards of American-style democracy and the free market economy ('shaping the Middle East'); or even that it is allegedly vital to save the Iraqi people from a bloody dictator, and to protect the United States from the supposed alliance between the Baathist regime and al Qaida. This Orwellian accumulation makes it hard to distinguish the processes that have been at work for about a decade and which crystallize at the start of this war.

Whatever it is, this ideological endeavour takes into account the need felt by the strategic system to establish the legitimacy of the Iraq War both internally and internationally, in order to avoid the accusation of tyranny. The war is conducted according to radical technological methods, by perfecting maximum synergy between ground and air forces with those in space. However, the awesome American military machine is 'humanized' by the work of 'embedded' journalists; in this way, a curious thing is created, a real new media, which brings alive the daily life of war and American soldiers in front of the world's television cameras, who treat the ongoing war according to the techniques of reportage and 'reality TV'. This results in the euphemistic portrayal of the technological power that is pulverizing the Iraqi State and its army, in favour of a perspective suitable for individual human experience.

The reality of war thus acquires a dimension which is hardly more dramatic than that of most television programmes. Its harshness, the implacable Nature of very experienced professional soldiers, is rendered better by cinema than 'live' programmes. Antoine Fuqua's film recalls this rawness ruthlessly, by showing that war is not conducted by machines, but by men and that, by definition, it cannot be either 'clean' or 'surgically precise'. On the other hand, the Nature of war changes dramatically according to its status as a 'just' or 'unjust' war. In the film, the just war, according to the American system of values, is conducted in order to protect a specific people, in particular from the threat of genocide, and it sets out this cause as the most enlightened and positive aspect of American political culture.

In doing so, the film comes to upset the security system's attempts to formulate and establish beliefs in people's minds. The movie is at the junction of militant militarism which has cut across American society since the 1950s, but which has experienced a crisis since the attacks of September 11, and a virulent critique of all wars conducted for arbitrary reasons. The army is in this way presented as the entity in which the politically fundamental conflicts of American civilization are played out, and it is by the political and ethical endeavour within the soldiers themselves that the risk of tyranny can ultimately be averted, insofar as it is already potentially present within the institution and inspires the behaviour of the chain of command.

However, the film has a more fundamental political scope. The Bruce Willis character, followed not long after by his men, suffers a profound shock by discovering the reality of genocidal war, even though he is himself an extremely remorseless military professional. This shock makes him lose his professional position, and takes him back to the world of the '*zoon politikon*', of the 'social animal', which only attains its founder political dimension of the human estate by an acceptance of discovering himself in the gaze of another. In this case, the Africans that he decides to save.

Now, this aim goes radically against the heavy-handed approach which cuts across the American military machine, and which is embodied at the individual level by the Defense Secretary Donald Rumsfeld. In effect, the significance underlying the promotion of space power, and the electronic and reticular renewal of the doctrine of 'lightning war', expressed by the 'shaping the Middle East' strategy and the conquest of Iraq, originates in the process of seeing the American system impose its standards on the countries it occupies, without suffering the effects of interaction. This strategic dream would make the United States a quasi-demiurgic power whose absolute strategic superiority would allow them to cut themselves off from phenomena proper to all forms of exchange between human societies. In doing so, the American strategic system is driven by a deep-seated tendency to divide humanity into 'them' and 'us', which fundamentally challenges any idea of universal humanism. *Tears of the Sun* goes against this philosophy. Cinema sheds light on these profound tensions in the strategic debate and the reactions to which they give rise.

### Resistance or Revolution?

The emphasis placed by the over-represented neo-conservative wing of American strategists within the administration of George W Bush on technological superiority magnifies a process which is relatively difficult to identify: the gradual autonomization of, the most technologically advanced parts of all organizations, particularly the military in this case. This tendency, brought about by the automatic nuclear warning systems of the Cold War, has grown to such an extent that questions are being asked about the need for possible political action.

These problems are at the heart of *Terminator III*, a vehicle for, and partly produced by, Arnold Schwarzenegger, who was keen to recover his international celebrity status before launching his campaign to be the Governor of California. The film charts the final few hours before the end of the world. The young John Connor, now aged about 20, has been living in hiding since the death of his mother, whom he saved years previously from the Terminators, who were sent from the future to kill the head of the human resistance fighters against the genocide begun by the machines at the start of the twenty-first century. He encounters at the same time a protector terminator, reprogrammed by the resistance members of the future, and a redoubtable female terminator, programmed by the machines. Whilst John Connor and his girlfriend battle to survive, the centre of the US Air Force responsible for updating cyber war software and robotic combat equipment is preparing to introduce the Sky Net super programme. This software is extremely powerful and is authorized to take control of all of the US army's IT activity, in order to coordinate them better. The protector terminator manages to lead Connor and his girl friend to a former government atomic bomb shelter where the female terminator sacrifices itself just at the moment when Sky Net takes control of the nuclear arsenals. In order to free itself from human control, it launches nuclear strikes both against the United States and the other nuclear powers to trigger off a chain reaction. The film ends on the destruction of American towns and cities and by the desperate radio appeals of National Guard units to the government headquarters which is empty apart from two young people, who know that their Destiny will be to have to organize the resistance and live in the horror of a world devastated by and subjected to genocide.

Curiously, although Arnold Schwarzenegger follows the screenplay closely, he also breaks the taboo of 11 September, and puts forward a serious charge against the American nuclear position, and a vitriolic discourse against the reality of the current strategic threat. The first half of the film takes place in Los Angeles, where the confrontation of the two terminators leads to the collapse of the fronts of apartment blocks, fires and police and firefighters being overwhelmed. This urban pandemonium is one of the very rare cinematic allusions to the 11 September attacks.

What the film brings out strongly is that the dislocation of daily life implied by the war results from the confrontation between forces that escape 'normal' and normed categories, understanding the world, and around which is expressed the consensus with which a society determines its reality. While the war breaks out, its actual rationale is only grasped on condition that comprehension of the world thus far is abandoned. These phenomena are illustrated by John Connor's disbelief right up to the point where the world blows up.

In addition, the massacre of humanity by Pentagon software and material raises the dilemma of the contemporary vacuity of political power in relation to extreme power, but also to the fragmentation of military power. The American State at the beginning of the twenty-first century is shown as an empty seashell, while the armed forces are suffering from hubris, the pride of men who think they are gods, and whom the latter always punish with destruction.

*Terminator III* is thus a national security fable, which develops not just according to the current combat activities in which America is involved, but by closely following the pursuit of automation that has long been driving the research centres of the American armed forces. This tendency starts moreover to become publicly noticeable with the deployment of observation and combat drones in Afghanistan and Iraq, with the updating of combat aircraft controlled remotely from a jet fighter with a human crew, the increased use of terrestrial drones in combat zones, but also in the near future, on and under the sea. What is more, while the film brings the power of IT and nuclear power into contact, it also makes reference to the amalgamation at the end of 2002 of Strategic Command and Space Command. This amalgamation, decided for administrative reasons, in the context of the struggle between the Defense Department and the new Department of Homeland Security, leads to the creation of a 'pool' of technological skills, the consequences of which are extrapolated by the film. Also, somewhat bizarrely, the film which is given the responsibility of launching Arnold Schwarzenegger's political career and charisma reaches the same conclusion and ends in the same way as *Doctor Strangelove* 40 years previously, despite the Cold War being at an end. On the other hand, the source of the real threat remains a military machine that is in the process of being dehumanized, which is badly controlled by its own chain of command, and virtually ignored by the executive and judiciary, at a time when the military budget is undergoing unprecedented increases.

This increase in power of the national security system also inspires, as we have seen with these two films, a willingness to resist. This process is found in certain screenplays because of the polarization of American political life brought about by George W Bush's presidency. The calling into question of many civil liberties in the name of security, but especially the radicalization of conservative traditions, and the most liberal sections of American society feeling besieged once again, begins what in the United States is known as 'culture wars' – the ongoing conflict between visions of the world, which dates back to the first days of the colonization.

In this way, the Jacksonian tradition which drove the conquest of the West, the deportation and extermination of indigenous American Indians, is based on the idea of religious and racial superiority, on steely conservatism and uncompromising behaviour towards all enemies. It endures still particularly in the Southern States and restarted the confrontation with all the liberal overhangs promised by the successors to northern political liberalism handed down from the eighteenth century and the American Revolution. The stakes of the new relationship being constructed between the United States and the rest of the world since Bush Jr's nomination for the presidency, the 11 September attacks and the wars that followed, have led to a deep identity crisis in the heart of this already very divided society. This division is seen in the split within the strategic debate between those in favour of developing an authoritarian, militaristic and prescriptive America towards its allies, but also towards any country deemed important to US strategic interests.

The liberal tradition's 'entering into resistance' towards the conservative and unilateralist offensive is expressed in the revival of films about Classical antiquity, like Wolfgang Petersen's *Troy*, with Eric Bana and Brad Pitt, and Antoine Fuqua's *King Arthur*, starring Clive Owen and Keira Knightley. The first film depicts the Greek coalition, united by King Agamemnon's imperialistic ambitions, who lays siege to the eastern city of Troy, whose leaders aspire only to peace and commerce.

The director puts forward a profoundly disenchanted vision of Homer's epic: the gods are no longer statues worshipped by visionaries, and the hero Achilles fears his name will be forgotten. The war, which is remarkably filmed, questions America's current identity. Is it like the predominantly peaceful city of Troy, which leads a defensive, therefore just, war against 'barbarous invasions'? Or rather are Americans these same barbarians who will devastate the east, blinded by pride, imperialism, militarism and greed?

The answer to this question is inspired by a deep pessimism: the eastern city of Troy, like the Greek coalition, is annihilated in the final battle. This battle begins by an asymmetric attack, with the trap of the Trojan Horse. It is important to note that Troy's most religious faction decide to bring the horse into the city, which is presented by the Greeks as an offering to Apollo. It is therefore the pious men, those who interpret history and politics in terms of signs which express the divine will, who cause the loss of the city, civilization, and the smooth running of daily life and peace. As for the Greeks, who are supposed to be the people who began the spread of Western civilization, they are shown as being intrinsically Machiavellian, and their leaders are possessed with a vision of the world which divides humanity between the strong and the weak. However, the quasi end of the world that is the fall of Troy leads to the survival of a group of Trojans, while the Greeks lose their leaders, Achilles and Agamemnon, who embody their power and imperialism, but also their aspiration to transcendence.

The film in fact comments on the disenchantment of American Destiny, which is losing its exceptional Nature, while the Republic moves towards a system of conquest, arbitrariness and a downward spiral into brutality, which takes it into wars from which it emerges irredeemably weakened, even 'demeaned'.

This setting of the film in the context of the invasion and occupation of Iraq embraces not only the political and philosophical dimension of the debate around this question, but also the depths of the problem posed by the definition of military identity. The two main characters are Hector, son of Priam, King of Troy, and Achilles, a minor Greek king and warrior of immense talent. These two men embody the two sides of the warrior ethic. One prepares for war and fights to defend his city and protect his wife and child. The other is filled with the intoxication of battle and glory and by contempt for political leaders who seek out power and hegemony.

The film explores the two facets of this 'warrior mentality' because if soldiers are required to wage war, war can only be won by those who sublimate this condition to become men who discover their *raison d'être* in combat and victory, and are just as prepared to kill as be killed. This predilection for sacrifice alone makes fighting effectively possible.

*Troy* thus fits in with American preoccupations that have developed from the end of the 1980s, where the national security system has been trying to perfect an armed force capable of responding to the challenges of an increasingly violent world and where its authority was always contested. It is in this context that Robert Kaplan, the travel journalist who was very much struck with a tragic vision of history, formalized the debate with his articles and book on the need to rediscover the 'Pagan ethos'. At the same time, the US Army launched the curious research and development programme whose aim was to recreate a 'warrior ethos' in order to turn the mentality of American soldiers away from the idea of career, like an armed civil servant or military bureaucrat, and promote one in which not only violence, but also sacrifice and the idealism of bearing arms, was rediscovered. This programme is a reaction to the ideology of 'zero losses', which has a tendency to create a distance between soldier and combat, notably by an over-reliance on technology. Like Troy, if the city is not protected by its own warriors, it is destined to fall to the cunning and might of barbarous warriors.

This problem is reprised and taken further in *King Arthur* (2004), whose astonishing complexity fits into the American strategic debate at the same time, while proposing radical solutions to the paradoxes which are pushing the US strategic system towards a deep crisis, and whose repercussions are felt the world over.

The legend of King Arthur is rewritten in historical fashion, putting the fifteenth-century legend in the context of the emergence of events, men and problems of the sixth century, at the beginning of the oral tradition which immortalized the Knights of the Round Table. The film shows Arthur as a Roman centurion of Breton origins, heading a unit of Sarmatian warriors, which holds back incursions by the Woads from north of Hadrian's Wall. At the beginning of the film, Rome sends Bishop Germanius to bring back the son of a Roman noble, who has been chosen to be the next Pope, but who is trapped in his estate by a Guerilla group of Woads. The mission falls to Arthur and his knights, as vast numbers of Saxon troops arrive, seeking to conquer Brittany, while killing the local people like the Romans beforehand. Arthur finds himself organizing the Roman evacuation to the south, to save a young Woad princess from being killed by fanatical Roman catholics, while avoiding being caught by the Saxons. The deadly threat represented by the Saxons leads the Sarmatian knights, Arthur and the Woads to form a common front.

This alliance is helped by Arthur's political and religious beliefs. Arthur is a follower of the Roman Christian philosopher Pelagius, who maintained that all men are equal in the eyes of God, contrary to Bishop Germanius, who had him executed, convinced as he was of the superiority of the Catholics of Rome over the pagans. His mission accomplished, Arthur turns his attentions towards the Saxons and remembers he is above all a Breton and faced with the threat of extermination hanging over his people. He is accompanied by his knights, Guinevere, the Woad princess, who is the daughter of the druid Merlin. The final battle sees the death of Saxon chiefs, but also most of the Sarmatian knights. The film ends with the marriage of Arthur and Guinevere, and by the foundation of monarchy, which will be inspired by the principles of Pelagianism.

The problems developed in this work reflect the complexity of tensions that weigh heavily on American political and strategic identity. Basically, a process of delegitimization and weakening is shown using the time-honoured metaphor of Rome while the internal conflict about empire increases in strength, but also that the barbarians get and begin to knock it down. It is civilization itself which seems in danger. Civilization here is understood according to two fairly different meanings: at first, civilization is associated with Rome, City of Light (which also recalls the speech of the hero of *Gladiator* before the death of Marcus Aurelius, and to the appropriation by the American cinema industry of the 'City upon a Hill' myth), put another way, in terms of wisdom and peace. However, the Roman Catholic fanaticism and the monstrousness of the Saxons brings about a change: civilization becomes the State that allows the immigrant Roman population in Brittany to live together as equals with the local people, in direct contrast to the State of arbitrary and unbridled violence of the savage Saxons, where the only authority recognized is that of the warrior capable of imposing himself over others.

This concept goes back to the American myth according to which the society of the United States is a composite of exogenous and endogenous groups living in harmony and peaceful negotiation. But this myth is put to the test at the time when asymmetric warfare emerges when American strategy is exported internationally to the global level. In effect, the conflict between Catholicism and Pelagianism comes down to a conflict about religious definitions of nationhood, this shared worship of the American project as the intervention of Providence. The question is, faced with the development of and splits in the American nation, whether the definition of the latter is open, or closed to, the standards it upheld from the end of the nineteenth century to the end of the twentieth century. What is more, these movements towards dislocation are reinforced by the fear aroused by the increasingly violent reactions that 'America' inspires in many parts of the world.

In this way, since 2003, Samuel Huntington is being reinstalled at the centre of the conservative establishment's production of ideology, with the extension of his 'Clash of civilizations' theory in his work, *Who are we?*, which declares that the profound demographic changes brought about by Hispanic immigration and others are in the process of modifying both the balance of power and the definition of the American nation. Implicitly, it is the decline in political force of the wasp population and their oligarchies which is evoked, although it was they who defined the nation.

These conflicts of identity are expressed in the film by the inter-community tensions where Arthur assumes the role of strong-arm negotiator by intervening between the aggressive factions of each social group. But this generalized dislocation is resolved by recourse to the strategy of asymmetric warfare, that is to say the confrontation between the weak and the strong, the Breton and Sarmatian 'guerillas' against the vast Saxon army of invasion.

The invasion of Brittany is treated as the medievalist metaphor of the encounter between the Viet-Cong or special forces, and the Anglo-American armada of 'The Longest Day', and transformed into a gang of blond and barbarous Nazi forerunners, allowing the director to create a genuine ideal type of representing what is an asymmetric confrontation. In this way, the first encounter between the Breton-Sarmatian and the Saxon forces is a battle between eight knights, and 200 heavily-armed Saxon soldiers on a frozen lake. Yet the victory belongs to Arthur and his companions, because he succeeds in disrupting the Saxons by using longbows, and by a form of 'eco-tactic', breaking the ice with axes, causing the Germanic warriors to drown. The 'weak' also manage to overcome the 'strong' by using the size and weight of their opponents against them, all while avoiding direct contact.

This scene is part of cinema history, taking up again as it does the finale of Eisenstein's *Alexander Nevsky* (1938), which portrays the victory of the 'weak' Russian army, led by the founder of the Russian State, Prince Alexander, against the fearsome Teutonic knights from Prussia, who are both Catholic and destructive. It must not be forgotten that Eisenstein's film was produced against the backdrop of the 'great patriotic war' of the Soviet Union against the Nazis.

This 'asymmetric' military and environmental victory, made possible by the mobilization of Russian citizens, is reprised by Hollywood in the context of the re-evaluation of the State of American identity confronted with its new enemies.

There is something surprising in the choice of enemy. While today, the enemy is identified with clandestine networks capable of preying on society's weaknesses, here it is likened to the massive strength particular to the Germanic people in Europe, between the Middle Ages and the twentieth century. The film thus expresses the sense of extreme strategic decline felt by the United States, and by those movements who are looking to find a way for it to be re-established, to the extent where the foundation of the British monarchy is envisaged as a golden age, the imagined memory of which becomes a source of inspiration.

What is more, underlying this comment are deep layers of American strategic recall, and the memory of how American power developed between the mid-nineteenth and mid-twentieth centuries, by challenging Germanic influence. The short-lived victory of Americanization over the Germanization of the world in 1945 is reworked as the victory of civilization over barbarism, and humanism over genocide, and presents American history as capable of re-establishing the nation by just war.

## Strategic Identity

While the production of *King Arthur* was coming to an end, Edward Zwick's *The Last Samurai*, starring Tom Cruise, was released. This very fine work fits in to the as veiled as obvious disalignment of large parts of Hollywood with the hard line of Washington, despite the director's moderate Republican commitments in his previous productions.

By taking an actual episode from the (forced) opening up of Japan to trade with the United States and the major imperial European powers, Zwick is involved in the Hollywood machine's latest appropriation of actual events to produce a virtual and alternative history. The film follows the progress of the experiences of a cavalry captain, played by Tom Cruise, who, fresh from the civil war and fighting with the American-Indians, is eaten away by the memory of atrocities and massacres he has witnessed and in which he has participated. With other American officers, he is hired by the Japanese defence minister, in order to help modernize the imperial army. In Japan, he organizes rifle and cannon training, before being involved in an expedition against a group of rebel Samurai warriors who are opposed to the policy of modernization. The soldiers, armed with modern equipment, are massacred, and the captain is captured; he then finds himself in the midst of a rural community of warriors and peasants, where he gradually discovers spirituality, and, as a prisoner, becomes the friend of the rebel Samurai chief. The chief is in revolt because he believes using Western military technology will lead to dishonour and the loss of the essential values of his country, something which, in social terms, is expressed by the disappearance of the Samurai caste. *The Last Samurai* ends with an extraordinary battle during the forces of State's offensive against the Samurai, which is won as the warriors charge, swords aloft, against the machine guns and cannon. It is a massacre, and the victory of the State is paid for with inexpiable dishonour. The political and psychological shock is such that the Emperor himself realizes the risk run by Japan of losing its soul, and declares that 'he dreams of a united and peaceful nation' – recalling both Abraham Lincoln and Martin Luther King!

Edward Zwick's film is on a collision course as much with current American strategic events as with the tensions of identity which traverse State and society. His imagined story of asymmetric war (of 'strong' and 'weak'), where a modern, over-equipped army, dominated by the American model of using crushing firepower, brushes aside a small band of warriors from a non-industrialized society, and who are ineffective as long as they cannot engage in man-to-man combat, but who are still fearsome, instantly echoes the methods employed in the Iraq War. Similarly, the Samurai's nocturnal incursions, or their use of the environment and lightning strikes make them redoubtable adversaries, who force the imperial State into disproportionate reactions that take away its legitimacy.

But this evocation of asymmetric war is part of the genealogy of American strategic history, and indissociable from its foundation by conquest, because of the genocide of American-Indian populations by the US army. The Indian wars end in 1890 at Wounded Knee, when the last Cheyenne warriors are massacred by machine gun. This founding event of American military supremacy over the places where it is deployed is at the heart of the cinematic account, which poses the question of knowing if this strategic history is not also the loss of some fundamental values, because it established the reign of State bureaucracy and technology over the creation of close social ties, in the context of which life, in harmony with others and with Nature, takes on its whole meaning. On the other hand, adopting the Western model amounts to the loss of 'Manifest Destiny'.

This film opposes the realist concept of a State's power politics with a more idealistic concept. At a time when American strategic efficiency is being neutralized by the occupation of Iraq and the development of resistance to it, sustained as much by the brutality of ground and air forces, as by the solidarity of Iraqi families when they lose one of their number, which justifies their behaviour by ideals they scorn. In this context, the film takes on an essentially political dimension, which, after *Glory* and *Under Siege*, is considered to be representative of American military policy. But it demonstrates that from now on, the strategy and fundamental values of the United States have virtually become antinomical.

This denunciation of the risk of dehumanizing and disintegrating the social ties linked to an inexorable rise in power of the national security system and technological security measures is shot through *Equilibrium*, with Christian Bale and Emily Watson. In a post-nuclear war world, an Orwellian society has developed, ruled by the omnipresent figure of 'The Father', where everyone is subjected to a daily chemical treatment, so as to become emotionless and maintain order in the city. The corps of 'Clerics', who are at the same inquisitors, elite police and exterminators of subversive elements, especially track art smugglers, because works of art trigger off far too much emotion. The most effective of the 'Clerics' gradually stops taking his treatment, realizes that he has come to deny his humanity by abandoning love, and becomes the leader of the revolutionary forces.

The film shows the organic link between security forces, electronic surveillance devices and repression by making the 'Clerics' dehumanized figures, even more effective than robots would be. What is more, this institutionalized organization of society in church/barracks comes back to the representation of American society as a 'nation whose soul is a church', as well as 'Fortress America'. The film envisages the way in which civilian religion can be perverted, and, instead of preserving the democratic ideals they have adopted, become the cult of anti-humanistic security values. Faced with this deviation, the only solution envisaged becomes the recourse to revolution.

It is this problem of revolution which reaches its crisis point in the radical political phenomenon that is Michael Moore's work, *Fahrenheit 9/11*, the *Palme d'Or* winner at the Cannes Film Festival in 2004. This film (not a documentary!), in the guise of an anti-George W Bush satirical tract, explores the way in which, according to the director, the American political classes come from the most ruthless oligarchies, which only have the sense of their own interests, but never that of the national interest. On the contrary, according to Moore, the American people has seen itself robbed of power by an illegitimate elite, who manipulate the middle and lower classes, orchestrated along racially discriminatory lines. The only solution, implicitly (but quite clearly!), would be to revolt. This implication lies in the title and elsewhere, which recalls Ray Bradbury's *Fahrenheit 451*, the description of a totalitarian society in which firefighters are ordered to burn piles of clandestine books and works of art. But one day, a fireman begins to read, organizes a resistance network, and begins a revolution. It is noteworthy that this book was adapted for cinema by Franois Truffaut, the book and the film being well known to Michael Moore, which he recognizes at Cannes, something which reinforces France's function as the essential relay of trans-nationalizing the American national strategic debate!

Michael Moore supports his argument with an icy sociological analysis of the State of the American army, by showing to what extent the young soldiers are lost and incapable of seizing the sense of their presence in Iraq, all while engaging in breathtaking military violence, because they struggle to differentiate between their job and a play activity. In so doing, Michael Moore, joins *Tears of the Sun, Troy, Equilibrium* and *The Last Samurai* in denouncing the deviation of the armed forces into dangerous militarism, which is made possible by the loss of all civic and humanistic spirit in the heart of the armed forces, who serve the illegitimate factions who hold the reins of State power.

These doubts about the orientation of American strategy and the historic directions being taken amplifies American civilization's particular tendency to envisage the emergence of threats they would not be able to face up to, and which would condemn them to extinction.

## Genocide and Extinction

The foreign policy of invading Afghanistan and Iraq, but also of withholding the American signature on numerous international treaties, the homeland security policy, and the spiral of hatred, resentment and suspicion that is set off in the rest of the world, as much in non-aligned countries as among old allies, leads to profound political and philosophical turmoil. This discord reactivates the feeling of vulnerability inherent in the perception that American society has of itself, and which is expressed in the significance of the problem of genocide, and by the fear of physical extinction.

The question of genocide cuts across *Tears of the Sun, Terminator III, Equilibrium, Arthur, Troy*, and *The Last Samurai*. The omnipresence of this theme is inscribed in the calling into question of the legitimacy of American policy, whose very existence is consubstantial with 'original sin', the genocide of American-Indian populations between the end of the eighteenth century and the start of the twentieth century. The very fact that the American nation was created by genocide establishes the idea and the fear that the United States could one day come to a brutal end. What is more, the Americans particular conviction of belonging to an exceptional nation leads them to very ambivalent positions between the willingness to adopt an exemplary foreign policy and to implant the idea that instances of genocide must be prevented everywhere, and the American State's own interests, which are not in risking its men in complicated Third World conflicts.

In addition, the notion of genocide has a powerful metaphoric content in American political language. Genocide is associated with Nazism. Hitler, the modern figure of evil, was defeated by American forces, as are the allies of Satan by the real believers who conform to the most rigorous Christian ideals.

Asking the question about the relationship to genocide is therefore asking about absolute evil, and the position adopted by the American system faced with this threat. This also amounts to asking about the potential capacity of this system of attaining sanctity, something which is illustrated by the Christ-like figure of Bruce Willis at the end of *Tears of the Sun*, after he has saved a small group of people from genocide.

It is against this highly-charged political, religious and semantic backdrop that Roland Emmerich's *The Day After Tomorrow*, was released, starring Dennis Quaid and Jake Gyllenhaal. The problem of genocide here veers towards an even more radical direction perhaps, that of extinction. The film follows a radical climatic shift because of global warming: the melting of the Arctic polar ice cap saturates the Gulf Stream with cold water as it keeps the northern hemisphere in a temperate climate. *The Day After Tomorrow* is one of the most audacious, subversive and courageous national security films of the last 20 years. It treats, by way of fable, the catastrophic effects for the United States and the world of the possible effect of current global warming, which would be the setting off of a new Ice Age across the northern hemisphere. In order to safeguard a part of the American population, the federal State launches a mass evacuation towards Mexico, who will only open her borders in exchange for Latin-American debt being wiped out. Meanwhile, a climatologist searches for his son who is stuck in the ice-bound Central Library in New York. On the other hand, the population of the northern United States is left to its fate, the blindness of politicians forcing them into this choice through powerlessness.

Contrary to the tradition of national security films, who make the American strategic system the vehicle for the material and spiritual salvation of the United States, the film does not show any miracle solution: the survival of the United States is only ensured by the solidarity of the 'Third World' with the 'First World' and by that between the generations, individuals, the sexes, single people and families, and, finally, between scientists, politicians and the military. Implicitly, the very notion of competitiveness, then, explicitly, that of the form of anti-ecological capitalism which had led to the catastrophe, is ridiculed by the survivors.

The subversive dimension of the film stands in the portrayal of this relativization of American power and its driving force: the United States is, effectively, infinitely dependent upon the rest of the international community, and their fate, like that of all developed countries, is subject to unknown factors of the climate. Climate escapes all demonstration of strategic force, because it is an autonomous power, to which there is no other choice but to submit oneself after changing it by the irrational exploitation of natural resources. The film therefore deals with the forced abandonment by Americans of their exceptional country, which ceases to be one of 'Manifest Destiny'.

The end of this mentality is illustrated by the refusal to use military power, as if the 'Good America', which has abandoned arrogance and sense of superiority, was neither violent, militaristic nor exceptional. The extinction of half the American population is combined with that of people living in the northern hemisphere and thus becomes the extinction of the fate-like spirit of 'Manifest Destiny'.

This 'renaissance' comes back to the vitality of the Biblical culture in the United States. The United States, for having adopted economy over ecology, is subjected to a new 'Flood', and forced to cross the Rio Grande, the new Jordan, in order to attain the Promised Land. Buildings act as arks and the survivors will construct a more harmonious world, bathed in a transcendental light.

But this new America is from now on linked to by a 'bridge of ice' to Europe and Russia, which obliges it to rediscover the importance of the rest of the world, and the global community who prescribe the fate of humanity. This need for global awareness is emphasized by the images of the half-frozen planet, taken from the International Space Station.

This astonishing work therefore makes use of stereotypes from national security films, and turns them on their head by creating solidarity and recognition of the interdependence of 'everyone together', the State of the future of humanity, which depends on the adoption of a cooperative global model.

But, despite this fairly optimistic ending, the film comments above all on a global process that American power can only make worse, and which threatens the US with extinction. This threat is itself metaphoric: the fear depicted here is the loss not only of physical but also spiritual integrity, on which the religion of 'Manifest Destiny' rests. To suffer global warming like every other nation, amounts to admitting that the United States is only one of many power bases, in particular faced with those emerging in the South, and in Latin America which, until the end of the 1980s, remained the 'private hunting ground' of the national security system and major US companies. It is therefore America's international status, but also its understanding of itself through its strategy, that is currently being played out.

# CONCLUSION

For more than half-a-century, US strategic history has also been that of a whole section of cinema which has extended actual history by creating a world of images and thus a mental universe where American strategic identity is established as one of the essential facets of national identity. The sense of being an elected people and conducting just wars are united in this national identity or become it because of the power of cinematic representation.

This tendency has been particularly deep-rooted since the war in Iraq in March 2003. Unlike the Gulf War of 1991, it can be filmed because it appears legitimate in the eyes of the American public and Hollywood. But, at the same time, relations between the political and strategic powers and those in cinema are entering into a new era where it becomes difficult to establish how the structural links and interdependence that up until now united Washington and Hollywood are going to evolve. While the major studios are quietly adopting a certain autonomy towards politics, the role they have assigned themselves to give a heroic and sacred image to the national security system has been strengthening virtually year on year since 1996 and *Independence Day*.

There was a major parting of the ways in this development with the war in Iraq. Like all sections of American society, cinematic production is alive to the ideological atmosphere which has surrounded the United States since the attacks of 11 September 2001. New forms of American strategy could generate a certain suspicion, but this will not be expressed openly by cinema, which is finding increasingly spectacular material in military expeditions and in the accumulation of ever-more sophisticated technological means of domination.

This tendency coincides with a portrayal of France which, for a number of years, has been worrying from a Gallic perspective: either France is completely out of the picture, as in *Independence Day*; or Paris is destroyed, as in *Armageddon*; French people can just as well be members of a neo-Nazi nuclear conspiracy in *The Sum of All Fears*, or again appear as ambiguous 'allies', full of cunning and duplicity, in *The Patriot*. At best, the south of France becomes an agreeable holiday resort for James Bond and sundry American agents, once their missions are accomplished.

There is a fear that this image is not getting better as time goes by because American cinema will continue to portray new strategic threats and to develop an alternative universe where American strategy is both glorified and questioned by its practical applications. The audience and the international impact of this type of cinema are such and determine to such a level the image that Americans and the rest of the world make of the US that make it vital to follow the way in which the country has developed in national security cinema.

# POSTSCRIPT

## *Alexander*, neo-Messianism and neo-conservatism

The re-election of President George W Bush in November 2004 was one way of expressing the fundamental importance of questions of identity in the United States today. One strong trend in the current creation of national identity is powerfully defined by Sebastien Fath as that of 'neo-Messianism', an ideology that no longer only identifies America with the result of a Divine plan but which makes the US a power with Divine attributes. 'America' becomes the religion of the United States, and tends to replace the traditional relationship with transcendence in increasingly large sections of society. This age-old disposition is currently in the process of expansion and magnification.

This tendency is expressed notably by the world vision popularized in so-called 'neo-conservative' circles in Washington, which makes 'America' out to be a fundamentally benevolent power, the secularized and immanent version of the 'City upon a Hill', which can therefore only do Good, and whose strategy is about putting this ontological positivity into action. It involves a secular relationship with the immanence of America, articulated to a desire to adapt the world to American interests and needs, which is well expressed in the 'shaping the Middle East' ideology.

The different ways of applying this ideology are expressed, in particular, by the destruction of Saddam Hussein's Baathist regime, the occupation of Iraq and by extensive re-organization plans forced on the Muslim world, from Morocco to Afghanistan, so as to convert these countries to democracy AND TO the free market American model, while surrounding the world's main oil resources at the same time. Oliver Stone's *Alexander* appears in this context. The film, starring Colin Farrell and Angelina Jolie, retraces the conquering King of Macedonia's youth and upbringing, his campaign against King

Darius of Persia, his flight in Central Asia and India, relations with his close circle and his death in Alexandria.

The 'Greek' world vision is developed at length: according to the philosopher Aristotle, Asia is made up of 'inferior races' and 'barbarians', and invasion of the continent amounts to giving its people the gift of 'freedom'. The conquest of Asia Minor as far as Egypt is viewed as a 'liberation' of barbarians enslaved to the Persian despot. These military advances, then the famous battle of Gaugamela, which allows Alexander to seize the Persian throne, are shown from an eagle's perspective. This symbol *par excellence* of American power illustrates both the vigour, purpose, nobility and implacable character of the spread of this 'young' power in an Asia so ancient that it has become incapable of change.

The victory is also shown as that of a light army, clearly inferior in number to the 'Asian masses', but whose mobility and modernity are strategic advantages that nothing can withstand.

We find here again the whole problem of the 'transformation' of the American military machine, which aims to make the US army a flexible tool, whose speed and fire-power are the means of outclassing any adversary. what is more, the 'Greek' political and strategic administration is presented as an elite of men, united by the links of friendship and an ancient common upbringing, a love for their charismatic leader, a homosexuality understood as a form of initiation and fraternity, and the certainty that they uphold both superior values and titanic myths, in particular that of Achilleus, Heracles and Prometheus, the 'friend of man', who gives them the necessary vision and strength to change the world order. This titanic dimension corresponds to their self-belief in one 'Greek' faith, and in the certainty that anything is possible, if sufficient individual and collective will is mustered. This universe of possibilities is embodied in reality by the strategic process that will create an 'empire of freedom and light', but also a conquering of self. Alexander, who symbolizes the America that likes to think of itself as able to 'illuminate the world', constantly repeats to his close friends and relations, 'Conquer your fear and you will defeat death itself!' It is therefore as much about a mystical quest as a strategic project. This intertwining of the spiritual and the political/military, peculiar to the neo-Messianism of the neo-conservatives, is however conscious of its limits.

The dream a 'union' of 'West' and 'East is shattered when the momentum of the advance is interrupted, because of Greek exhaustion, and the resistance of Indian princes. Military victory is no longer sufficient, when the 'Orientals', all of whom are remarkably treacherous, refuse Western values. This refusal is seen in the last battle of the film, whose violence is such that it uses up even Alexander and the Greeks psychological reserves, while the

Indians have enough men to sacrifice to recommence the fighting. This reversal is expressed by the screen becoming red, illustrating the potentially endless bloodbath that is opening up as the only future for the conquerors. Contrary to the way in which television treated September 11 by refusing to show blood, thus the nation's mortality, the 'projection of force' on Eurasia therefore risks to destroy the myth, literally by cutting its throat, just as Alexander sacrifices the Bull in order to gain the favour of the Gods.

This project and failure are nonetheless considered via the 'myth' that spurs on the conquest, and is considered as valid in principle, this 'failure, which far surpasses successes'. Nevertheless, the death of Alexander, which is also that of the ideal, is presented like the victory of separation, of 'Asian sorcery', then of disenchantment, and gives way to increasing numbers of wars and the emergence of new powers. This film conveys a profoundly tragic political and historical philosophy because the only way peace can win out over weapons would be for men's spirit to be able to free itself from its 'narrow-mindedness', to embrace the imminent values from the 'West'. But even the conquerors are incapable of doing this. However, this impetus towards glory, and the pursuit of liberty by force and myth, are shown as justifying the enterprise in itself, and symbolize an America which does not recognize any limits imposed on it from the outside, despite its inherent risks.

# NOTES

## 1 – National Security Cinema

1   Michael Rogin, *Ronald Reagan, The Movie, and Other Episodes in Political Demonology*, Berkeley, University of California Press, 1987, introduction, p.1.
2   *Sun Tzu on the Art of War: The Oldest Military Treatise in the World*, trans Lionel Giles M.A. (1910) quoted on numerous Internet sites.
3   During the 'American cinema and American military strategy' conference organized by Jean-Michel Valantin at the Postgraduate School of Social Sciences (EHESS) in France, 24 May 2000.

## 3 – Justifying the New Strategic Power

1   Paris, La Découverte, 1994.
2   Edgar Morin, *La Méthode*, vol. 4, *Les Idées: leur habitat, leur vie, leurs moeurs, leur organisation*, Paris, Le Seuil, 1991
3   Quoted in Frances Fitzgerald, *Way Out There in the Blue: Ronald Reagan, Star Wars and the End of the Cold War*, New York, Simon and Schuster, 2000, p. 191.

## 4 – New Threats

1   Henry Kissinger, hearing before the Armed Forces Commission, in *Crisis in the Persian Gulf Region: US Policy Options and Implications. Hearings before the Committee on Armed Services United States Senate, One Hundred First Congress, Second Session, 11, 13 September, 27, 28, 29, 30 November, 3 December, 1990*, Washington DC, US Government Printing Office, 1990, p. 293.
2   Ibid, p. 327.
3   Pierre Clastres, *Le Grand Parler: mythes et chants sacrés des Indiens Guaranis*, Paris, Le Seuil, 1974, and *Recherches d'anthropologie politique*, Paris, Le Seuil, 1980.
4   Samuel Huntington, *The Clash of Civilizations and the Remaking of World Order*, Touchstone, 1997. The French edition was published in 1997 by Odile Jacob under the title, *Le Choc des Civilisations*.

## 6 – Pearl Harbor Syndrome

1   Cf. *Le Monde*, March 17 2003.

## 7 – Saving Ground Combat

1    Carl von Clausewitz, *De la guerre*, Editions de Minuit, Paris, 1955.

## 9 – The State and Defence

1    Geoffrey Peret, *A Country Made By War*, New York, Random House, 1989.

# FILMOGRAPHY

*Abyss*, James Cameron, 1989; starring Ed Harris, Mary-Elizabeth Mastrantonio, Michael Biehn.

*Air Force One*, Wolfgang Petersen, 1997; Harrison Ford, Gary Oldman.

*Alien*, Ridley Scott, 1979; Sigourney Weaver, Tom Skeritt.

*Aliens*, James Cameron, 1986; Sigourney Weaver, Michael Biehn, Tom Paxton.

*Alien III*, David Fincher, 1992; Sigourney Weaver, Charles Dance.

*Alien: Resurrection*, Jean-Pierre Jeunet, 1997; with Sigourney Weaver, Winona Rider.

*Apocalypse Now*, Francis Ford Coppola, 1976; with Martin Sheen, Marlon Brando.

*Armageddon*, Michael Bay, 1998; Bruce Willis, Ben Affleck, Liv Tyler.

*Blue Thunder*, John Badham, 1983; Roy Scheider, Malcolm MacDowell.

*Clear and Present Danger*, Phillip Noyce, 1994; Harrison Ford, Willem Dafoe.

*Commando*, Mark L. Lester, 1985; Arnold Schwarzenegger, Rae Dawn Chong, Dan Hedaya.

*Contact*, Robert Zemeckis, 1997; Jodie Foster, Matthew McConaughey.

*Courage Under Fire*, Edward Zwick, 1996; Denzel Washington, Meg Ryan, Scott Glenn.

*Crimson Tide*, Tony Scott, 1995; Denzel Washington, Gene Hackman, Viggo Mortensen.

*Dead Zone*, David Cronenberg, 1983; Christopher Walken, Martin Sheen.

*Deep Impact*, Mimi Leder, 1998; Tea Leoni.

*Die Another Day*, Lee Tamahori, 2002; Pierce Brosnan.

*Die Hard*, John McTiernan, 1988; Bruce Willis, Bonnie Bedelia.

*Die Hard 2*, Renny Harlin, 1990; Bruce Willis.

*Die Hard: With a Vengeance*, John McTiernan, 1995; Bruce Willis.

*Dr Strangelove*, Stanley Kubrick, 1963; Peter Sellers, George C. Scott.

*Enemy of the State*, Tony Scott, 1998; Will Smith, Gene Hackman, Jon Voigt, Barry Pepper.

*Escape from LA*, John Carpenter, 1996; Kurt Russell.

*Executive Decision*, Stuart Baird, 1996; Kurt Russell, Steven Seagal.

*Fail Safe*, Sidney Lumet, 1964; Henry Fonda.

*Firefox*, Clint Eastwood, 1982; Clint Eastwood.

*GI Jane*, Ridley Scott, 1997; Demi Moore, Viggo Mortensen.

*Gladiator*, Ridley Scott, 2000; Russell Crowe, Connie Nielsen, Joaquin Phoenix, Richard Harris.

*Glory*, Edward Zwick, 1990; Denzel Washington, Morgan Freeman, Matthew Broderick.

*Godzilla*, Roland Emmerich, 1997; Matthew Broderick, Jean Reno.

*Goldeneye*, Martin Campbell, 1995; Pierce Brosnan, Sean Bean.

*Independence Day*, Roland Emmerich, 1996; Will Smith, Jeff Goldblum.

*In the line of fire*, Wolfgang Petersen, 1993; Clint Eastwood, Rene Russo, John Malkovich.

*Invasion of the Bodysnatchers*, Don Siegel, 1956; Richard Widmark.

*Invasion of the Bodysnatchers*, Philip Kaufman, 1978; Donald Sutherland.

*Invasion of the Bodysnatchers*, Abel Ferrara, 1993; Forest Whitaker.

*Invasion USA*, Joseph Zito, 1985; Chuck Norris.

*JFK*, Oliver Stone, 1991; Kevin Costner, Tommy Lee Jones.

*Lethal Weapon*, Richard Donner, 1987; Mel Gibson, Danny Glover.

*Lethal Weapon II*, Richard Donner, 1989; Mel Gibson, Danny Glover, Joe Pesci.

*Lethal Weapon III*, Richard Donner, 1991; Mel Gibson, Danny Glover, Rene Russo.

*Lethal Weapon IV*, Richard Donner, 1997; Mel Gibson, Danny Glover, Jet Li.

*Little Big Man*, Arthur Penn, 1970; Dustin Hoffman, Faye Dunaway.

*Logan's Run*, Michael Anderson, 1976.

*Minority Report*, Steven Spielberg, 2001; Tom Cruise.

*Mission: impossible*, Brian de Palma, 1995; Tom Cruise, Jean Reno, Vanessa Redgrave.

*Mission: impossible II*, John Woo, 1999; Tom Cruise, Ving Rhames.

*Moonraker*, Lewis Gilbert, 1979; Roger Moore, Michael Lonsdale.

*Murder at 1600*, Dwight Little, 1996; Wesley Snipes.

*Nixon*, Oliver Stone, 1995; Anthony Hopkins, James Woods, Paul Sorvino.

*On the Beach*, Stanley Kramer, 1959; Gregory Peck, Ava Gardner.

*Patriot Games*, Phillip Noyce, 1992; Harrison Ford, Sean Bean, James Earl Jones.

*Pearl Harbor*, Michael Bay, 2000; Ben Affleck, Kate Beckinsale, Josh Harnett.

*Planet of the Apes*, Franklin J. Schaffner, 1968; Charlton Heston.

*Predator*, John McTiernan, 1987; Arnold Schwarzenegger, Carl Weathers.

*Predator II*, Stephen Sommers, 1990; Danny Glover, Bill Paxton, Gary Busey.

*Rambo*, Ted Kotcheff, 1982; Sylvester Stallone, Brian Donnehy.

*Rambo II*, George Pan Cosmatos, 1985; Sylvester Stallone, Richard Crenna, Charles Napier.

*Rambo III*, Peter MacDonald, 1988; Sylvester Stallone, Richard Crenna.

*Reign of Fire*, Rob Bowman, 2001; Christian Bale.

*Red Dawn*, John Milius, 1984; Patrick Swayze, Vincent Spano.

*Red Heat*, Walter Hill, 1988; Arnold Schwarzenegger, James Belushi.

*Rocky IV*, Sylvester Stallone, 1985; Sylvester Stallone, Dolph Lundgren.

*Rollerball*, Norman Jewison, 1975; James Caan.

*Rules of Engagement*, William Friedkin, 2000; Samuel L. Jackson, Tommy Lee Jones.

*Salvador*, Oliver Stone, 1986; James Woods.

*Saving Private Ryan*, Steven Spielberg, 1998; Tom Hanks, Tom Sizemore, Matt Damon, Barry Pepper.

*Small Soldiers*, Joe Dante, 1997; Elijah Wood.

*Space Cowboys*, Clint Eastwood, 2000; Clint Eastwood, Tommy Lee Jones, Donald Sutherland, James Garner.

*Spy Game*, Tony Scott, 2001; Robert Redford, Brad Pitt, Catherine MacCormack.

*Starship Troopers*, Paul Verhoeven, 1997; Casper Van Diem, Denise Richards.

*Star Wars Episode IV – Star Wars*, George Lucas, 1977; Mark Hamill, Harrison Ford, Carrie Fisher, Alec Guinness.

*Star Wars Episode V - The Empire Strikes Back, Irvin Kershner, 1980; Mark Hamill, Harrison Ford, Carrie Fisher, David Prowse.*

*Star Wars Episode VI – Return of the Jedi*, Richard Marquand, 1983; Harrison Ford, Mark Hamill, Carrie Fisher, David Prowse.

*Superman*, Richard Donner, 1978; Christopher Reeve, Gene Hackman.

*Superman II*, Richard Lester, 1980; Christopher Reeve, Gene Hackman.

*Swordfish*, Dominic Sena, 2001; John Travolta, Halle Berry, Hugh Jackman.

*Terminator*, James Cameron, 1984; Arnold Schwarzenegger, Linda Hamilton, Michael Biehn.

*Them!* Gordon Douglas, 1954; Rod Taylor.

*The Art of War*, Christian Duguay, 1999; Wesley Snipes, Michael Biehn.

*The Beast*, Kevin Reynolds, 1988; Ethan Hawk.

*The Bourne Identity*, Doug Liman, 2002; Matt Damon.

*The Contender*, Rod Lurie, 2000; Joan Allen, Jeff Bridges, Gary Oldman.

*The Day After*, Nicholas Meyer, 1983; James Coburn.

*The Day the Earth Stood Still*, Robert Wise, 1951; Robert Taylor.

*The Hunt for Red October*, John McTiernan, 1990; Sean Connery, Alec Baldwin.

*The Invisible Man*, Paul Verhoeven, 1999; Kevin Bacon.

*The Matrix*, Andy and Larry Wachowski, 1998; Keanu Reeves, Carrie Anne Moss, Lawrence Fishburne.

*The Osterman Weekend*, Sam Peckinpah, 1983; Rutger Hauer, John Hurt, Burt Lancaster.

*The Peacemaker*, Mimi Leder, 1997; George Clooney, Nicole Kidman.

*The Rock*, Michael Bay, 1995; Nicholas Cage, Sean Connery, Ed Harris.

*The Second Civil War*, Joe Dante, 1997; Dan Hedaya.

*The Siege*, Edward Zwick, 1998; Denzel Washington, Annette Benning, Bruce Willis.

*The Sum of All Fears*, Phil Alden Robinson, 2001; Ben Affleck and Morgan Freeman.

*The Tailor of Panama*, John Boorman, 2000; Pierce Brosnan, Geoffrey Rush, Jamie Lee Curtis.

*The Time Machine*, George Pal, 1960; Rod Taylor.

*The War Game*, Peter Watkins, 1965.

*Thirteen Days*, Roger Donaldson, 2000; Kevin Costner.

*Three Kings*, David O. Russell, 1999; George Clooney.

*Tomorrow Never Dies*, Roger Spottiswoode, 1997; Pierce Brosnan, Michelle Yeo.

*Top Gun*, Tony Scott, 1986; Tom Cruise, Kelly McGillis, Val Kilmer.

*Traffic*, Steven Soderbergh, 2000; Benicio del Toro, Catherine Zeta-Jones, Michael Douglas.

*True Lies*, James Cameron, 1993; Arnold Schwarzenegger, Jamie Lee Curtis, Bill Paxton.

*Under Siege*, Andrew Davis, 1992; Steven Seagal, Tommy Lee Jones.

*Under Siege 2: Dark Territory*, Geoff Murphy, 1995; Steven Seagal.

*Village of the Damned*, Wolf Rilla, 1960.

*Volcano*, Mike Jackson, 1996; Tommy Lee Jones, Anne Heche, Don Cheadle.

*Wag the Dog*, Barry Levinson, 1997; Dustin Hoffman, Robert de Niro.

*Wargames*, John Badham, 1983; Matthew Broderick, Peter Coyote.

# BIBLIOGRAPHY

Arendt, Hannah, *Essai sur la revolution*, Paris, Gallimard, 1967.

Artaud, Denise, 1995, *Les Etas-Unis et leur arriere-cour, la defense de la troisieme frontiere*, Paris, Hachette.

(The United States and their Backyard: the Defence of the Third Frontier)

Baritz, Loren, 1985, *Backfire, A History of How American Culture Led Us to Vietnam and Made Us Fight the Way We Did*, John Hopkins University Press.

Boyer, Paul, 1985, *By the Bomb Early Light, American Thought and Culture at the Dawn of the Atomic Age*, New York, Pantheon Books.

Bowden, Mark, 1999, *Black Hawk Down, A History of Modern Warfare*, New York, Atlantic Monthly Press.

Bromley, Simon, 1991, *American Hegemony and World Oil, the Industry, the State System and the World Economy*, Cambridge, Polity Press.

Brzezinsky, Zbigniew, 1997, *Le Grand Echiquier, l'Amerique et le reste du monde*, Paris, Bayard.

(The Great Chess Board: America and the Rest of the World)

Burrows, William E, 1998, *This New Ocean, The Story of the First Space Age*, New York, The Modern Library.

Campbell, Duncan, 2001, *Surveillance electronique planetaire*, Paris, Editions Allia.

(Electronic planetary surveillance)

Clausewitz, Carl von, 1995, *De la guerre*, Paris, Editions de Minuit.

(On War)

Davis, Mike, 1997, *City of Quartz*, Paris, La Decouverte, Paris.

Duclos, Denis, 1994, *Le Complexe du loup-garou: la fascination de la violence dans la civilisation americaine*, Paris, La Decouverte.

(The Werewolf Complex: the Fascination for Violence in American Civilisation)

Elias, Norbert, 1975, *La Dynamique de l'Occident*, Paris, Calmann-Levy.

(The Western Dynamic)

Engelhardt, Tom, 1995, *The End of Victory Culture*, New York, Free Press.

Fitzgerald, Frances, 2000, *Way Out There in the Blue: Ronald Reagan, Star Wars and the End of the Cold War*, New York, Simon and Schuster.

Freedman, Lawrence, 1989, *The Evolution of Nuclear Strategy*, New York, Saint Martin's Press.

Frodon, Jean-Michel, 1999, *La Projection nationale*, Paris, Odile Jacob.

(National casting)

Gordon, Michael R., and Trainor, Bernard E, 1995, *The General's War, the Inside Story of the Conflict in the Gulf*, Boston, Little Brown and Co.

Halberstam, David, 1969, *The Best and the Brightest*, New York, Ballantine Books.

Huntington, Samuel, 1997, *Le Choc des civilisations*, Paris, Odile Jacob, Paris.
(The Shock of Civilisations)

Jervis, Robert, 1989, *The Meaning of Nuclear Revolution, the Symbolic Nature of Nuclear Politics*, Cornell, Cornell University Press.

Kaplan, Fred, 1983, *Wizards of Armageddon*, New York, Simon and Schuster.

Koppes Clayton, Gregory D, 1987, *Hollywood Goes to War: How Politics, Military and Propaganda Shaped World War Two Movies*, New York, The Free Press.

Laurent, Eric, 1991, *Tempete du desert*, Paris, Olivier Orban.
(Desert Storm)

Luttwak, Edward, 1989, *Le Paradoxe de la strategie*, Paris, Odile Jacob.
(The Paradox of Strategy)

Morin, Edgar, 1991, *La Methode*, volume IV, *Les Idees: leur habitat, leur vie, leurs moeurs, leur organisation*, Paris, Le Seuil.
(Method: Ideas; their Habitat, their Life, their Customs, their Organisation)


Perret, Geoffrey, 1989, *A Country Made By War*, New York, Random House.

Pike, John, and Stambler, Eric, 1996, *Space Power Interest*, Boston, Westview Press.

Rogin, Michael, 1987, *Ronald Reagan, The Movie, and Other Episodes in Political Demonology*, Berkeley, University of California Press.

Rosenbaum, Jonathan, 2000, *Movie Wars, How Hollywood and the Media Conspire to Limit What Films We Can See*, Chicago, A. Cappella Press.

Slotkin, Richard, 1992, *Gunfighter Nation, the Myth of the Frontier in Twentieth Century America*, New York, Atheneum.

Sun Tzu, 2000, *L'Art de la Guerre*, translated by Jean Lévi, Paris, Hachette.
(The Art of War)

Weber, Max, 2002, *Le Savant et le politique*, Paris, 10–18.
(The Wise Man and the Politician)

Weber, Max, 1996, *Sociologie des religions*, Paris, Gallimard.
(Sociology of Religions)

# INDEX OF FILMS

# INDEX